CHILES AND SMOKE

Brimming with creative inspiration, how-to projects, and useful information to enrich your everyday life, Quarto.com is a favorite destination for those pursuing their interests and passions.

First Published in 2023 by The Harvard Common Press, an imprint of The Quarto Group, 100 Cummings Center, Suite 265-D, Beverly, MA 01915, USA. T (978) 282-9590 F (978) 283-2742 Quarto.com

The Harvard Common Press titles are also available at discount for retail, wholesale, promotional, and bulk purchase. For details, contact the Special Sales Manager by email at specialsales@quarto.com or by mail at The Quarto Group, Attn: Special Sales Manager, 100 Cummings Center, Suite 265-D, Beverly, MA 01915, USA.

23 24 25 26   1 2 3 4 5

ISBN: 978-0-7603-7811-3

Digital edition published in 2023
eISBN: 978-0-7603-7812-0

Library of Congress Cataloging-in-Publication Data

Names: Prose, Brad, author.
Title: Chiles and smoke : BBQ, grilling, and other fire-friendly recipes with spice and flavor / Brad Prose.
Description: Beverly, MA : Harvard Common Press, 2023. | Includes index. | Summary: "In Chiles and Smoke, pitmaster and professional recipe developer Brad Prose turns up the heat for smoky and savory barbecued meats, seafood, and vegetables"-- Provided by publisher.
Identifiers: LCCN 2022031774 | ISBN 9780760378113 (hardcover) | ISBN 9780760378120 (ebook)
Subjects: LCSH: Barbecuing. | Smoking (Cooking) | Outdoor cooking. | LCGFT: Cookbooks.
Classification: LCC TX840.B3 P76 2023 | DDC 641.7/6--dc23/eng/20220817
LC record available at https://lccn.loc.gov/2022031774

Design: Kelley Galbreath
Cover Images: Brad Pose
Photography: Brad Pose, except on page 6 which is by Jack Sorokin Photography

Printed in China

Brad Prose

CHILES AND SMOKE

BBQ, GRILLING, AND OTHER

Fire-Friendly Recipes

WITH SPICE AND FLAVOR

HARVARD
COMMON
PRESS

CONTENTS

FOREWORD

I FIRST FOUND BRAD THROUGH his recipe posts on social media. I was immediately drawn to his style, imagery, and creative recipes. A few comments back and forth eventually led to emails. Fast forward a bit and I realized I was talking to Brad a few times a week about recipe ideas, cooking, and, well, life in general.

I was drawn to Brad's uncanny ability to believe the best about people—and to help bring out their best. His level of faith in humanity is something that you cannot help but appreciate. I believe that is why he loves to cook: he not only wants to make delicious food, but to share it in a way that helps people feel loved. This is no small task, but he finds a way every single day to make that happen, whether it's with his family or through his recipes online.

Yet that's probably not why you have this book in your hand! To that end, never underestimate Brad's cooking knowledge. He is a lifetime student of the flame, making sure to put in long, hard hours to make some truly revolutionary dishes. While some chefs take a day, Brad often spends weeks trying to perfect some slight detail, from his Butterflied Chicken Drumsticks to Barbacoa Sauce. He is always on the hunt to make dishes that pop in flavor and explore new ground. This is, for me, what

Chiles and Smoke is all about: it's Brad's inventiveness on paper.

Having read through this cookbook many times (and, to be honest, having listened to him work on it every single day for the last year!), I can say it really is something to get excited about. Brad has found a way to combine his love of grilling and barbecue, his passion for chiles, and his inspiration from his family and friends into a single work of art. Recipes like the Enchilada Wings or the Gochujaung Chile Con Carne show how he can take an approachable recipe and pack it full of flavor.

His exploration into how to utilize chiles for the smoker and grill will open your mind and maybe even spark your own inventiveness. And it does not stop with the main recipes! Brad shares key rubs, sauces, and garnishes like Fresh Chili Powder from scratch, Guajillo Ketchup, and Pickled Jalapenos. In short, he makes sure that after going through this cookbook, you will have everything you need to excel over the flames.

Having sat in a front row seat for much of Brad's recent journey, I am truly honored to call him a friend. His heart for people and passion for delicious food are a perfect combination. He pushes me to grow into a better cook, friend, and human every day. So I'll leave you with this:

- May this cookbook inspire you to take bold leaps with confidence in your cooking.

- May it empower you to try new dishes knowing they had been tested with care.

- And may it also show you that you too can bring people together, just like the author.

—DEREK WOLF, *Over the Fire Cooking*

INTRODUCTION

LEARNING TO COOK FOR A VEGETARIAN was one of my greatest challenges as a young man. I still remember my wife when she was my new girlfriend. She chose not to eat meat, leaving me staring at the wall with no obvious options to impress her. At that time, I was the average backyard griller with very little cooking experience. I was raised by Midwest parents eating meat and potatoes. What the heck was I going to cook for her?

Most of my food journey up to this point was centered on a cheap gas grill, purchased from the local grocery store. Friends would bring over steaks knowing that I'd happily fire them up. Cooking for larger groups meant I would pull out all the stops, wrapping handfuls of wood chips into a sheet of foil to create some smoke.

Well, it turns out this new person in my life opened my eyes in more ways than one. I soon found there are a lot of options for vegetarians, and I quickly discovered how flavorful many of them were. My wife is Mexican, so that's where my food journey started to expand in the home kitchen as well. I spent a lot of time researching, learning how to make traditional sauces, salsas, and tortillas from scratch. Indian cuisine uses a lot of similar spices and chiles, which was another avenue of flavor for us. Middle Eastern recipes found their way into the house, and suddenly I realized we had many more food options.

Fast-forward a few years to the point where we were newlyweds. I had a low-paying job at the time, but I really wanted to upgrade the ten-year-old gas grill and buy a smoker. My wife wasn't completely opposed to the idea, but it was certainly a major expense. After months of searching online, I was able to bring home a used kamado grill.

Smoked briskets, ribs, and pork shoulders were soon flying off the smoker, filling up our fridge with piles of leftovers. The barbecue was good, and getting better over time, but I was starting to lose my excitement. We were still preparing very flavorful, globally inspired meals at home, and here I was warming up my salt-and-pepper brisket to eat with a bowl of chana masala. Separately the food was fantastic, but it wasn't connecting.

During these years, I learned from many cookbooks and also watched more hours of cooking shows than I could count. I'm glad I did. My major epiphany actually came from an episode of *The Mind of a Chef* on PBS, featuring Chef Edward Lee. He shared his food journey and philosophies, focusing on the fact that he views American food as limitless. People bring together their culture, recipes, and ingredients to establish their own local cuisine in creative ways. Hearing this for the first time was like having Chef Lee smack me in the back of the head.

Rather than casting aside certain combinations as inauthentic fusion, I ran with the idea that ingredients from different cultures can and should come together. There was no reason to feel constrained by a particular school of barbecue. Embracing the concept of limitless flavors, I took inspiration from the dishes I cooked for my family using chiles and a heavy hand with spices, bringing those flavors to the smoker and grill. Smoked barbacoa lamb leg stands out as one of the first recipes where this clicked. But as you flip through this book, you'll find many more from my journey.

The idea that there could be just about any combination of ingredients to create delicious food was burned into my mind. This concept of "limitless" flavors propelled me on an immediate journey straight into the kitchen. Most of the food I was interested in cooking for the family used a multitude of chiles and was heavily spiced, which translates very well into the world of barbecue. Keep flipping the pages to see how the evolution of my culinary journey around the globe continues.

CHILES AND SMOKE

There's a geographical concept called *cooking with latitude*, a way to find natural flavor pairings across the world using temperate zones. Consider how Phoenix and North Africa are similar, both sharing a taste for spicy chiles, warm aromatics, citrus, and herbs. Many of the ingredients are exactly the same. Those that are not can be simply swapped or adjusted and suddenly, you have something new and exciting with a similar flavor profile. This concept can be used for any location and cuisine around the world.

Cooking through global cuisines revealed to me that chiles are one of the most common and transferrable ingredients. A challenge of being a home cook is the lack of access to specific ingredients, especially when you're trying to cook food from around the world. Living in the Southwest, we have access to a wide variety of chiles, fresh and dried, but not necessarily what a recipe is calling for. As a recipe publisher, I was driven to find new combinations of flavors, with components easily accessible to the public while paying respects to the culture.

I set about educating myself on tradition, planting my focus on learning the authentic recipes and flavors that the world has to offer. Much of my focus was looking outside of barbecue and grilling, into comfort and street food for inspiration. From there, it was a matter of testing new combinations of chiles and spice to create flavors I hadn't experienced before. I wrote this book to share my flavorful food journey and many of the exciting recipes created along the way.

HOW TO USE THIS BOOK

- **DON'T LIMIT YOURSELF TO THE RECIPE YOU'RE READING.** Seasonings, marinades, and sauces can be used with other meats and vegetables. My goal is to expose you to different flavor combinations you might not have thought about.

- **CHILES ARE NOT *JUST* SPICY.** They are bitter, sweet, smoky, nutty, and much more. All of these recipes are largely designed to complement the food, not overwhelm it, so don't be afraid to swap salsas or sauces as you see fit.

- **MOST OF THE RECIPES USE KOSHER SALT,** which has an ideal coarseness for grilling and barbecue. Fine sea salt is used for a few recipes, some sauces, and condiments, but I don't recommend swapping them interchangeably. The saltiness will vary, as this has been tested.

- **THIS BOOK HAS RECIPES FOR BARBECUE AND GRILLING,** two different cooking methods. There are many recipes that indicate "indirect cooking," a term that could be considered a form of barbecue as the food isn't being cooked directly over the flames. Most of these recipes could be prepared using a grill with a large enough area for indirect cooking, allowing you to sear when needed.

- **MOST DRIED CHILES ARE AVAILABLE ONLINE** if you don't have access to them locally. Read the descriptions of the commonly used chiles and feel free to swap based on similarities or your tastes.

- **ALL OF THESE RECIPES WERE COOKED MANY TIMES,** by myself and others. Some of them have taken years to develop, honing in on the most ideal combination of flavors for my personal taste profile. My biggest advice is to taste and adjust. Your personal preference for salt or spice might be different, so make sure you have that spoon or fork handy and keep tasting.

LET'S HEAT THINGS UP

FIRST, A WORD

The recipes in this book are grounded in two simple but amazing things: chiles and smoke. In this chapter, I'll share fundamentals on both topics that will make the rest of the book more enjoyable.

When it comes to chiles, it's hard to play favorites. There are so many delicious chiles used in cuisines around the world! Yet, this is a book rooted in the cuisine of barbecue. Over many years, I've found there are a handful of chiles that simply work with this type of food—whether that's as a component of a rub or sauce on the meat itself or as another element that pairs with it. Thus, my aim with this chapter is to cover the greatest hits. It's not a chile encyclopedia. It's a chile cheat sheet for those that are passionate about cooking with grills and smokers.

Which brings me to this: Chances are that if you've picked up this book, you've got a foundation of knowledge in grilling and barbecue already. So, this book doesn't do a complete rehash of the basics. (If you want more guidance, see the Resources section starting on page 184.) However, after the chiles section in this chapter, I will include some of my recommendations and standards when it comes to grilling, barbecue, and essential equipment. That will make sure we're all on the same page for the recipes.

GRILLING AND SMOKING

GRILLING

Light up the charcoal and throw meat on the grates! Many think of grilling as a style of cooking where the food is prepared directly over the coals. This is often true, and cooking directly over charcoal (or, sure, gas burners) will give you both charred and wood-fired flavors easily. Searing food over medium to high heat is a fast process, though much less forgiving than cooking low and slow. Certain foods, like steak, chicken wings, and shrimp, are cooked hot and fast over the coals to provide a balance of char and smoke. If you smoked them without any direct heat, they would very likely turn out *too smoky*.

That said, the great thing about cooking with grills is the ability to not only sear over fire, but also to cook indirectly. With a large enough grill, you can set the coals to one side and create an environment in which you can smoke, roast, and grill at the same time. Throughout the book, you'll see this referred to as the *2-zone cooking setup*, which uses both sides of the grill to prepare the food. Having a "cool zone" gives the chance for meat to warm up slowly or even be smoked. It also allows the meat to escape from the heat if the grill's heat is taking off too fast.

Most smokers have fairly reliable and consistent temperature zones, but grills work differently. Whether you are searing or cooking indirect, it's a challenge to determine how hot the coals really are unless you have an accurate thermometer. Firepits fall into this category, usually having no lid and just open flames.

Thankfully, there's a reliable method that simply uses your hand. Carefully place your hand about 4 inches (10 cm) from the lit coals and count the seconds. Measure how long it takes before you need to remove your hand (because it is starting to hurt!) and refer to the table at left. This method gives you a fairly accurate estimate of the temperature, allowing you to cook with confidence. Remember, with grilling and barbecue you don't need to be exact. This style of cooking is all about instinct and reacting when you need to. I believe it's important to get a feel for your grill and its temperatures. There are many times when you don't want to keep opening lids or fiddling with food for temperature checks. If you know your equipment and master your sense of temperatures, you'll be less reliant on technology (at least until the end), and you'll likely have a lot more fun cooking.

SMOKING

Low and slow, this is the way for barbecue. This cooking method involves indirect cooking that produces a low heat, with the smoke heating, drying, and flavoring the food at the same time. Most food is smoked between a temperature of 180–300°F (82–150°C), as anything past that will produce much less smoke. There are methods out there for "hot and fast smoking" between 350–400°F (180–200°C), but I've found those to yield results that are similar to roasting in an oven. Burning wood will always produce a certain smoke flavor, but very little at those temperatures.

HEAT	TEMPERATURE	TOLERANCE
Low	200–250°F (93–120°C)	10–12 seconds
Medium-Low	250–300°F (120–150°C)	8–10 seconds
Medium	300–350°F (150–180°C)	6–8 seconds
Medium-High	350–400°F (180–200°C)	4–5 seconds
High	400°F (200°C) and higher	2–3 seconds

There are many types of smokers available now, from the traditional offset to the popular pellet grills. Wood-burning offsets typically put out a stronger smoke flavor but take much more management and time. Pellet grills are generally consistent, allowing you to step away for longer periods of time. The smoke flavors are not as strong; however, technology has been improving greatly over the years, closing the gap. Large grills with the ability to have two zones of cooking temperatures are also a way to smoke food, though are mostly ideal for smaller items due to the logistics required for fire and temperature management.

You might see some recipes in this book that require you to smoke a smaller item of food, such as a whole head of garlic, and wonder if it's worth firing up your smoker. Many of these smaller recipes are best if you fire up the smoker and add them alongside other foods. Save your energy and time: Throw some of that garlic in while you are smoking a brisket. My feeling is that if there's room in the smoker, use it.

RECOMMENDED GEAR

1 Instant-Read Thermometer: This is one of the most important pieces of equipment in your arsenal. Having a high-quality probe can mean the difference between a medium-rare and medium-well steak if you're moving fast. I like to use thinner thermometers for delicate foods, such as shrimp and fish.

2 Grill Tongs: Click them twice every time you pick them up—it's the rule. Seriously, I recommend finding some that are longer, with teeth pointing inward. This will make it easier to grab all types of food.

3 Grill Mat: These can be metal or silicone, and either is a very handy tool to smoke smaller foods or anything that could fall through the grill grates. The wire mesh mats are ideal for transferring fragile food to and from the smoker, such as bacon or jerky.

4 Cedar Planks: Wood grilling planks, not just cedar, can be used to infuse food with flavor while also keeping it moist. The planks are typically soaked in water ahead of time to prevent flareups.

5 Natural Fire Starters: Skip the lighter fluid. There are so many simple ways to light charcoal and wood without using chemicals. Many brands sell natural fire starters, which are generally wax-coated strands of wood fibers. In a pinch, greasy snack chips are high in fat and can do the job.

6 Cast Iron Skillet: Used over the coals or in the smoker, these versatile pans can do just about anything. You'll see them throughout the book for searing, braising, and even making queso. Try to find one with a lid if you can, as it will expand your possibilities.

7 Dutch Oven: Yes, there is some crossover with the cast iron skillet, but Dutch ovens allow for increased volume and better braising. These are ideal for low and slow chilis, stews, and braising meat for shredding. Make sure you have a lid for this, which will make everything much easier to manage.

UNDERSTANDING CHILES

PURCHASING CHILES

Fresh chiles are pretty straightforward, but there are a few tips to help you choose the best ones when shopping. Look for chiles that have a smooth skin, without the white cracks. Those white lines are referred to as *corking*, a process that happens when the inside of the pepper grows faster than the outside. The flavor of corked peppers will likely be more intense, both sweeter and significantly spicier.

When choosing dried chiles, look for ones that are still pliable and soft. They should also have a nice aroma, smelling of spice and dried fruit. Bend them slightly. If they snap or shatter from being brittle, they are more likely to be stale and bitter in flavor. Make sure you are choosing peppers that are whole, not broken apart.

PREPPING CHILES

There's no telling how hot a pepper is going to be until you taste it. It's easier to test fresh chiles for their heat by simply slicing off the tip and dabbing it on your tongue. You'll know this is a very spicy chile if it's already burning because it's the least spicy part of the pepper. The closer you slice to the stem, the hotter it gets.

An easy way to remove excess heat is to remove the membrane and the seeds from the chiles before cooking with them. Slice fresh chiles in half and then scrape out the white membrane and seeds. Dried chiles are trickier, as they should be fully hydrated with warm water before attempting to remove the tops and seeds.

To pull out the maximum amount of flavor from dried chiles, I recommend toasting them slightly for a minute or so before soaking. You can use the oven, but I prefer a hot, dry skillet which provides a bit more control. Don't let the chiles toast to the point of being black or they will be extremely bitter and burnt. Just cook them for 30 seconds or so on each side until you can start to smell them. Then, you can grind them up for chile powder or hydrate them with warm water and use them for sauces.

JALAPEÑOS

Medium-size, crunchy, juicy, slightly bitter

It all starts with jalapeños. They are, without a doubt, the most commonly used chile pepper in American barbecue. They taste delicious both raw and cooked, making them a staple for pairing with savory meats and grilled vegetables.

Jalapeños are known as the "fat chile" due to their plump shape. The flesh is much thicker than many other chiles, giving it that signature juicy crunch. They were named by the Spanish after the city Xalapa (or *Jalapa*), the capital of Veracruz. Historical records show the Aztecs cultivated them, and they smoked them into chipotles to preserve them. Mexico remains a major exporter of jalapeños, although you can also find them grown across the United States, India, China, Spain, and Peru. (I told you they are popular!)

Green jalapeños remind me of green bell peppers: juicy, bitter, and crisp. Spice levels vary greatly, so make sure you taste yours before adding it into a dish. Sometimes, you don't know if you're going to taste a fresh pepper or if you're going to absolutely blow off your taste buds. Leave a jalapeño on the vine long enough and they turn angry, changing into a bright red jewel. Fruity flavors start to peek through, the perfect pairing for the incredible heat. As red jalapeños are, as a rule, much hotter, they are typically used as a garnish, fermented into hot sauce, or as a measured addition to pickled vegetables.

Jalapeños are used throughout this book in a variety of ways to complement barbecue and grilling. Roasted

and peeled, they add a sharp punch to sauces such as the *Chile Verde BBQ Sauce* (page 135). One of my favorite flavor combinations in the book has to be pairing jalapeños with basil, which makes an incredible topping for grilled fish. It's hard to ignore the fact that classic *Pickled Jalapeños* (page 46) are in my fridge at all times.

CHIPOTLES
Smoky, fruity, tough skins

Red jalapeños left on the vine for a long enough time will lose their moisture. They can then be harvested, dried, and smoked to become chipotles. Their complex flavors have hints of tomato, cherry, and raisin. Two types of chipotle chiles exist: morita and meco. Morita chipotles are the most common in the United States, making up the majority of canned chipotles and packaged chile powders. These are tough yet pliable, smoked for half the time of the meco chipotle. Moritas have a sweeter flavor profile and a deep purple color. You'll recognize the differences right away, as the meco chipotle looks like a flattened cigar. These incredible smoky dried chiles have a sharp, earthy flavor. The morita chipotle chiles are used in this book, as they are the most accessible and recognizable for flavor.

These smoky and spicy chiles can be a backbone for flavor in barbeque, as they can add a complex layer of flavor to rubs and seasonings. Freshly ground dried chiles create a potent powder, adding an instant boost of deeper flavors in any dish. Hydrated in adobo sauce, they add a powerful punch when chopped or blended into stew, soups, sauces, or glazes. Personally, chipotles are one of my favorite chiles used with food cooked over the fire.

The flavor of chipotles can be very overpowering on their own, so it's important to find complementary ingredients that can round it out. Tomatoes work very well to carry the spice, such as the sauce from the *Smoked Chorizo*

Meatballs (page 130). Roasted garlic complements the chipotle, which you'll find in the *Spicy Garlic Mojo Sauce* (page 75), both ingredients having been transformed with deeper, roasted flavors. The ground chipotle chile powder creates a strong foundation when used in a rub, allowing food to have multiple layers of heat as you eat. My favorite example is the fiery *Nashville Hot BBQ Chicken* (page 95).

POBLANOS
Bitter, garden-fresh, earthy

Poblanos are some of the most versatile chiles over the fire, able to shine when used raw, roasted, and even puréed into sauces. Many Mexican and Southwestern dishes feature them as the main ingredient, from stuffed *chile rellenos* to creamy *rajas con queso*.

Poblano chiles are named after the state of Puebla where they were first cultivated. Quite large in size, they are fairly mild peppers when it comes to spice levels. Don't be surprised if you get that rare poblano with a spicy kick—it's happened to me more than a few times. Their flesh and skin are thick and dense, not nearly as crisp as a jalapeño or serrano chile. Typically, the skin is roasted and peeled, revealing the softer flesh on the inside. Most of the bitter flavors come from the skin as well, which is important to know for recipes that simply dice up poblanos before cooking.

Being larger in size makes them ideal for stuffing and grilling, the method used with *Bacon-Wrapped Cheesy Chicken Poblanos* (page 113). Charring poblanos is the most common way of using them, and it's incredibly easy. The skin needs to be blackened and scraped off, leaving you with the sweeter flesh. *Charred Poblano Pico de Gallo* (page 53) uses the soft poblanos to transform the flavors of the classic salsa. Roasted poblanos blend very smooth, making them an ideal choice to fortify a sauce.

ANCHOS
Fruity, smoky, mild sweet heat

Poblano chiles can be allowed to ripen to a bright red and then dried into ancho chiles. These are considered a foundation for many recipes in the Mexican and Southwest kitchens. These leathery, fruity-flavored chiles are dark brown in color with a hint of red. Once hydrated and puréed, the red intensifies and becomes a blood-red paste, which can be used for many different sauces.

Ancho chiles are known for their smoky and fruity flavors, producing a sweet heat. They smell like a combination of raisins and sun-dried tomatoes. Their spice level is pretty low, as any of the original poblano's heat has been tempered due to the drying process. You'll often find that ancho chiles are paired with other types of chiles to build a more complex flavor profile. Being sweeter in nature, they are an ideal component for pairing with smoked and grilled meats.

The *Arizona Adobo Sauce* (page 41) uses ancho chiles as the foundation, creating a flavorful paste. Use it as a marinade for chicken, shrimp, pork, or just about anything before throwing it onto the grill. Anchos pair well with other sweet flavors, such as orange, to create a well-rounded sauce. *Ancho-Orange Pulled Pork* (page 125) uses this sauce as a seasoning to finish the pork, creating a deeper flavor profile before being added into sandwiches or tacos. Dried anchos can also be ground into chile powder, providing a subtle smoky layer when making rubs and seasonings. They are the base ingredient for my staple seasoning, *Brad's Smoke Rub* (page 34), which is used throughout the book.

HABANEROS
Spicy, fruity, herbal

Bringing the heat, habaneros are my personal favorite when it comes to spicy chiles. I was converted after traveling to the Yucatán, eating bowls of different salsas made of all different varieties. These are the spiciest chiles you'll find in this book, but I find habaneros have a wonderfully fruity and floral flavor without being overwhelmed by the natural heat levels. That doesn't mean you should grab one and take a bite, as they have an aggressive burn that hits pretty hard and fast. These are chiles for which you *should definitely use gloves* when cutting them.

Habanero peppers are believed to have originated in Cuba and are thus named after the capital of Havana. They were given this name when traded with Mexico in the Yucatán Peninsula, where habaneros are now grown and widely consumed. It's related to the Scotch bonnet pepper, which means it does have some similarities in flavors and heat levels. In fact, habaneros grow all thorough the Caribbean, with slightly different characteristics in shape, color, and spice. The orange variety is the most common throughout the United States.

Did I mention these are pretty spicy? Habaneros are prized for hot sauce and spicy salsas. One of my favorite condiments is *Xnipec*, a spicy salsa from the Yucatán which inspired the recipe for *Hot Pickled Red Onions* (page 48). Charring the chiles brings out more of their heat, whereas pickling draws out the more fruity flavors. They pair particularly well with sweet dishes, building that sweet-heat profile while taming the spice levels. I love to infuse them into butter, such as the *Harissa Habanero Butter* (page 122) for a bold finishing move on pork, fish, or even vegetables.

GUAJILLOS
Spicy, smoky, tangy

Guajillo chiles are the second-most commonly used dried chile in Mexican cuisine, right after ancho chiles. They are slightly sweet, with a slight tang of cranberries. When toasted, the flavors become more complex with spicier,

smokier notes. Hydrated guajillos are typically combined with the fruitier ancho chiles and fortified with a spicier chile de árbol to create the most flavorful sauces and moles. Throughout the book, these chile combinations are used for marinades, rubs, and even barbecue sauce.

There are two main varieties of guajillo chiles. The most common is the longer and wider pepper seen throughout markets and in stores. This guajillo tends to have a fruitier, richer flavor with a mild heat. Harder to find in the United States, the *guajillo puya* is smaller and spicier. More spice companies have been bottling ground guajillo powder, as it's becoming well-known for its complex flavors with cooking.

One of my staple recipes is the unique *Guajillo Ketchup* (page 39), which uses guajillo chiles and tomatillos as the main ingredients, forming a complex sauce that is used throughout the book in various ways. The chile works well with sweet and acidic flavors, adding a layer of heat without overwhelming the other ingredients. Guajillo is used like this again with the *Tandoori Grilled Lobster with Lemon Parsley Aioli* (page 154), where it's equally important to have heat while allowing the meat flavor to shine through.

CHILE DE ÁRBOL
Very spicy, smoky, nutty
Milder than cayenne, but much hotter than a jalapeño, chile de árbol peppers find themselves right in the middle. They can be used as a fresh chile, and they grow pretty easily in the right conditions. But typically, these are sold as dried chiles, which are usually hydrated for sauces or ground into chile powder. Aside from the heat, they have smoky, nutty flavors that become more intensified when toasted or fried. Thankfully, these chiles don't immediately burn the tongue. The heat is delayed and lingers.

These chiles are native to Mexico, specifically regions in Jalisco. They were introduced to the United States and Southeast Asia through trade expeditions, hundreds of years ago. Dried chile de árbol peppers can now be found in different cuisines around the world including Caribbean, Pakistani, Thai, and many others. Just like other dried chiles, their flavor tends to change when toasted.

You might be wondering what this chile has to do with barbecue and grilling. Chile de árbol has the benefit of not being too spicy, yet still having a flavor that adds complexity to the dish. It also has what I think of as a delayed heat profile, which is ideal when creating seasoning blends, such as the *Spicy Chili Powder* (page 31). This staple seasoning can be used for chilis, fruit, barbecue rubs, or just about anything you can think of that needs that something special. There are two different chili recipes in this book, and I believe both benefit greatly from adding more piquancy to the flavor profile, especially *Smoked Sonoran Chili* (page 62), which tastes delicious on hot dogs, or corn chips, or anything really.

HATCH CHILES
Buttery, spicy, earthy, sharp
These seasonal chiles are highly sought after and celebrated, especially in the Southwest. Hatch chiles have a very unique characteristic. When roasted and peeled, the slightly bitter chile changes into a buttery, smoky flavor profile with an ideal balance between sweet and heat. Red and green Hatch chiles offer very different flavors as well as the reds presenting slightly sweeter.

Hatch chiles come from Hatch Valley in southern New Mexico, cultivating a passionate fan base throughout the state, as well as Texas, Arizona, and southern California. Every year, the reach seems to grow a little more, with online producers able to ship the Hatch chiles across the country. The annual Hatch Chile Festival draws in well over 30,000 attendees year after year to roast and consume these special peppers.

Their uses are almost unlimited, as they can be stuffed, puréed, ground, or chopped for different sauces and salsas. Hatch chiles have very strong natural flavors and don't require many ingredients to allow them to shine. The simple recipe for *Hatch Chile Smoked Shrimp Skillet* (page 151) requires a very small ingredient list, transforming the shrimp into a mouth-watering spicy dish. One of my favorite ways to use these chiles is to blend them with butter and a little kosher salt, a perfect topping for pork steaks, ribeyes, or roasted vegetables.

BELL PEPPERS
Sweet, bitter, earthy

Welcome the non-spicy chile to the table. Many varieties, from the bitter green to the small multi-colored, are some of the most versatile peppers across the world. The larger bell peppers are typically bitter in flavor when raw, sweeter when cooked. Smaller, sweet bell peppers have a much sharper flavor. From purées to pickled, a variety of bell peppers is used throughout the book to complement many dishes.

Bell-shaped peppers tend to fall into this category, regardless of their color. The most common are red, orange, yellow, and green, each with a slightly different flavor profile. I like to take advantage of the different flavors, combining them to make the *Brazilian Vinaigrette Salsa* (page 51), which can be paired with just about any grilled meat. The bitter and sweet flavors contrast with the charred, smoky profiles and create a really flavorful bite.

Mini sweet peppers pack a punch, concentrating all of that flavor with a sharp, sweet bite. They are typically consumed whole, rather than roasting and blending into sauces. I've found that grilling and pickling them maximizes their flavors, creating one of the best condiments for barbecue. *Pickled Sweet Bell Peppers* (page 45) can be used as-is or chopped up for other salsas and relishes.

SERRANOS
Spicy, sharp, citrus, crisp

Any time you need a bigger kick than a jalapeño, the serrano is the answer. These chiles have a sharp heat, with a dangerous delayed fuse. Give it a minute, and it really stings the tongue. Typically, you'll see them used for a variety of salsas, raw or cooked, or as a fresh garnish to brighten a dish. They tend to be quite juicy on the cutting board, which means that you better consider gloves when dicing. I'll never forget the experience of rubbing my eyes casually after cutting some serranos.

These chiles were named after the mountain regions in Mexico where they originated. Smaller and thinner than a jalapeño, their spice levels are much more concentrated. Typically, they are found in stores as a green chile, but if you're lucky (like me), you might live in a region where you can find orange, red, or brown colors, which will have slightly different flavors and heat.

One of my favorite ways to utilize them is to kick up salsa. The best fresh salsa in our house is the *Charred Poblano Pico de Gallo* (page 53), which utilizes fresh serranos alongside the bitter poblanos and bright tomatoes. Lime or lemon juice tends to tame the spice levels in salsas or marinades. This method is used with the *Lemon-Serrano Grilled Summer Squash* (page 175) to create a simple, flavorful oil to baste and season the veggies. If you're not sure how to use them, slice them into thin coins and slip them into your tacos for a spicy bite. You can't go wrong!

SHISHITO PEPPERS
Grassy, smoky, meaty, mild spice

Who can resist a bowl of charred shishito peppers? Move over edamame, this is the snack I crave. These chiles hardly take any work to prepare, and the flavors are so complex. Grilling or toasting them brings out the natural sweetness, softening them to the perfect texture. It's common practice to simply eat them whole, minus the stem. If you're like me, you are the one hoping to find that rare, very spicy pepper in every bowl.

Shishito peppers come from Japan, the name referring to the fact that the tip of the chile looks like a lion head (*shishi*, in Japanese). They have become so popular over the years that they are now widely grown across Europe and the United States. The plants are relatively easy to grow and produce several dozen peppers per plant, making them an ideal option to cultivate at home.

The most popular way to cook with shishito chiles is right over the fire, charring them on skewers and topping with a simple garnish. Bitter flavors from the peppers pair well with sweet heat as featured in the recipe for *Huli Huli Shrimp, Shishito, and Pineapple Skewers* (page 148). Their fibrous flesh makes them ideal for adding texture into dishes, especially when dicing them. Pairing them with a sweet, red bell pepper in the *Shishito Cheesesteak Queso* (page 81) elevates a typically creamy appetizer into a full-on meal. Feel like keeping it simple? Toss them over a hot skillet with a little oil until charred and then finish with salt and citrus.

KOREAN CHILES, GOCHUGARO, AND GOCHUJANG
Savory, spicy, toasted, sweet

I could probably write an entire book on gochugaru and gochujang: Korean chile powder and Korean chili paste.

These staples of the Korean kitchen have crossed over into the world of American barbecue, and I welcome them with open arms. The roasted, complex flavors of this Korean chile powder and paste add dimension and spice to a dish in a way that's so good but so easy, it almost feels like cheating.

Gochugaru is the dried, coarsely ground Korean gochu pepper. It is the main ingredient in the savory paste, gochujang. These chile flakes are much more that a one-note, typical crushed red pepper flake. Open the bag, and you're hit with smoky, fruity smells. The spice level is fairly mild, making this a safe alternative for those who shy away from very spicy foods. It's also a staple ingredient in kimchi, providing the signature heat and color. You'll find this used in my signature brisket rub, the *Firecracker Brisket Rub* (page 71), paired alongside aromatic spices such as Szechuan peppercorns and fennel for an explosion of flavors.

Gochujang paste has a special place in my pantry, and there are usually a few tubs of it. Made of gochu chiles, glutinous rice, fermented soybeans, and salt, this magic paste creates an irreplaceable flavor with incredible depth. It's a very savory condiment, similar to miso paste, with a "umami" flavor that pairs perfectly with just about anything related to barbecue. My *Gochujang Chili con Carne* (page 59) is fortified with this paste, paired with chipotles and jalapeños for a five-alarm flavor blast. It also works well as a marinade, right before hitting the grill, a technique used with the *Gochujang Honey Mustard Chicken Sandwich* (page 109). Try some of these methods, and you'll find out how easy it is to experiment in your kitchen.

MY PANTRY STAPLES
Every chef and home cook has their secret sauce, rub, or magic touch to sprinkle into a dish. These rubs, condiments, and sauces are essential in our home kitchen. You'll

find most of these recipes popping up throughout the book, used in a variety of ways. My goal is to make sure that if you're going to take the time to create any of these staple ingredients, you'll have options to use them. Adjust them to suite your tastes and preferences as needed.

FRESH
CHILI POWDERS

MAKES
ABOUT

1½

CUPS
(180 G)

I couldn't write this book without sharing my signature blends for chili powders. These are household blends regularly used for my tacos, chili, beans, and so much more. Walking in the local markets past the tables with mounds of dried chiles inspires me, smelling the aromas of spice, leather, and sweet fruit. One chili powder wasn't enough, so there are two varieties, providing flexibility depending on the recipe. You'll find them used throughout the book, but you should also try sprinkling these on fruit, dusting the top of your *Southwest Creamed Corn* (page 173), or mixing with some margarita salt for the rim of your glass. The applications are pretty much endless.

SPICY CHILI POWDER
8 dried chile de árbol peppers
5 dried guajillo chiles
5 dried chipotle morita chiles
1 tablespoon (6 g) cumin seeds
1 tablespoon (6 g) ground Mexican
    oregano
1 teaspoon fine sea salt
2 teaspoons garlic powder

LIGHT CHILI POWDER
4 dried ancho chiles
4 dried guajillo chiles
2 dried chipotle morita chiles
1 tablespoon (6 g) cumin seeds
1 tablespoon (6 g) ground Mexican
    oregano
1 teaspoon fine sea salt
2 teaspoons garlic powder

INSTRUCTIONS
Preheat the oven to 350°F (180°C, or gas mark 4). Place the whole chiles on a baking sheet and toast for 6–8 minutes until they are fragrant and brittle. Be careful not to burn them. You might need to check on the smaller chiles sooner.

Let the chiles cool and remove the stems and seeds. Tear the chiles into smaller pieces and add them, with the cumin seeds and oregano, to a spice grinder. Grind into a fine powder and stir in the salt and garlic powder. Store in an airtight container at room temperature for up to a month.

CHILE POWDER
OR
CHILI POWDER

CHILES ARE USED WIDELY throughout many different styles of cooking. It's only natural to find a variety of them in the stores. The challenge is that you don't always know what you're buying in the bottle.

Chile powders are ground dried chiles, and chiles are typically the only ingredient. You should know if you're buying guajillo, chipotle, or New Mexico chile powder because it should be clearly labeled on the bottle. The chiles could be toasted, but they potentially might have just been ground from their dried state.

Chili powder on the other hand is a blend of dried chiles and spices, which is not always obvious unless you look at the label. Typically, you'll also find at least garlic powder, salt, and cumin. It can vary greatly from there, with other "herbs and spices" mixed in. Trying different brands and blends is fun but can be frustrating when you're trying to refine your recipes at home.

Bottled ground chiles or chili powder can potentially be sitting on the shelf for a long time, which dilutes the strength of the natural flavor. This has a bigger impact on the more subtle chiles, such as ancho chiles, as opposed to the spicier chiles, such as cayenne, which aren't nearly as affected.

The best flavors are going to come from your spice grinder. Take the time to toast and grind your chiles or your chili powder blends. Your taste buds will love you for it!

SMOKY
COFFEE RUB

Dark coffee and steak have a magic bond when cooked together, tenderizing the outside and complementing the roasted flavors from wood-fired grilling. Many chiles have a natural bitterness, which works with the coffee and cocoa powder in this rub. Sumac is the secret ingredient: The tart, acidic flavors remind me of fresh lemon zest, brightening the flavors of the seasoning and the beef. Try this rub on any type of steak, such as ribeye, filet mignon, or even prime rib. Pair it with a topping of roasted chiles, such as the shishito gremolata in *Coffee-Rubbed Tri-tip with Shishito Gremolata* (page 69).

INGREDIENTS

2 tablespoons (28 g) kosher salt

1 tablespoon (6 g) fresh ground
   black pepper

1 tablespoon (5 g) ground
   espresso coffee

½ tablespoon ancho chile powder

½ tablespoon ground sumac

1 teaspoon granulated garlic

1 teaspoon Dutch process
   cocoa powder

½ teaspoon ground cinnamon

INSTRUCTIONS

Combine all ingredients in a small bowl. Stir well to distribute the ingredients. Store at room temperature in a sealed container for up to 2 months. The fresher the ground coffee, the longer it will last.

BRAD'S
SMOKE RUB

<table>
<tr><td>MAKES
ABOUT

2

CUPS
(275 G)</td></tr>
</table>

Sometimes, you just need a go-to jar of seasoning that will work on almost everything. This smoke rub is designed for low and slow barbecue, regardless of whether you're cooking beef, chicken, or pork. Base ingredients build the foundation of sweet and salty, fortified with the fragrant aromas of fennel, coriander, and cumin. Layers of chipotle and ancho build a subtle, smoky heat. This all-purpose blend of spices and chiles was designed to complement the flavors of the various sauces and garnishes used throughout the book. Plus, it makes the meat glow a pretty bright red, and that just looks cool.

INGREDIENTS

1 tablespoon (11 g) yellow mustard seeds
1 tablespoon (10 g) black peppercorns
1 teaspoon cumin seeds
1 teaspoon coriander seeds
1 teaspoon fennel seeds
⅓ cup (75 g) kosher salt
¼ cup (28 g) paprika
¼ cup (60 g) brown sugar
¼ cup (50 g) white sugar
2 tablespoons (18 g) ancho chile powder
1 teaspoon dried Mexican oregano
2 teaspoons granulated garlic
1 teaspoon chipotle chile powder

INSTRUCTIONS

Heat a skillet over medium heat on the stove. Toast the mustard seeds, peppercorns, cumin seeds, coriander seeds, and fennel seeds for a few minutes, shaking the pan until the seeds smell aromatic. Remove from the heat and allow them to cool.

Blitz the toasted spices into a rough powder using a spice grinder or coffee grinder. Mix with the rest of the ingredients. Keep in a sealed container at room temperature for up to 3 months.

SMOKED GARLIC
AIOLI

MAKES
ABOUT

2
CUPS
(450 G)

Chef Matt Deaton showed me a photo of his smoked mayo, a homemade ingredient he uses on his menu at Allman's Bar-B-Que in Fredericksburg. It's a subtle smoke flavor, able to be stirred into sauces, pasta salads, or simply slathered on a bun. He inspired me to create this *Smoked Garlic Aioli*, a similar concept that uses an entire head of smoked garlic as the foundation. The subtle flavors of roasted garlic and wood-fired smoke are brightened with a tang of red wine vinegar and lemon. You might think an entire head of garlic sounds overpowering, but the sharp flavors are tamed with the low and slow cooking process. Use this to make the most flavorful *Desert Deviled Eggs* (page 161) or even a burger sauce for the *Chiles and Smoke Burger* (page 57).

INGREDIENTS
1 whole garlic head, unpeeled
2 egg yolks
1 teaspoon Dijon mustard
2 teaspoons fresh lemon juice
1 teaspoon red wine vinegar
½ cup (120 ml) canola oil
¼ cup (60 ml) extra-virgin olive oil
Kosher salt and black pepper

NOTE: Use a food processor if you don't have an immersion blender. The steps are the same, adding the eggs, garlic, mustard, lemon juice, and vinegar into the processor. Start blending and slowly stream in the canola oil. Transfer the contents to a mixing bowl, whisk in the olive oil, and season to taste.

INSTRUCTIONS
Prepare the smoker for indirect cooking at 250°F (120°C).

Place the entire head of garlic on the smoker and allow it to smoke for 60–90 minutes, depending on how much smoke flavor you'd like. I like to do this while I'm cooking other food, taking advantage of the real estate in the smoker.

Peel the garlic cloves from the skins once cooled and place them into a Mason jar, wide enough to fit an immersion blender. Add the egg yolks, Dijon mustard, lemon juice, and red wine vinegar. Pour in the canola oil, but not the olive oil. Place the immersion blender into the jar and push it all the way to the bottom. Start to mix, leaving it at the bottom to grind up the garlic and slowly lift it up while running. The mixture will emulsify and thicken into a white sauce.

Transfer the contents to a mixing bowl. It's time to whisk in the olive oil, rather than blending it, which can make a bitter flavor. Whisking constantly, slowly stream in the olive oil. Season with salt and pepper to taste. This will last in the fridge for up to 2 weeks.

GUAJILLO
KETCHUP

MAKES
ABOUT

2

CUPS

(720 G)

Trust me, this is a ketchup worth making from scratch. Tangy flavors from the tomatillos and vinegar might remind you of a barbecue sauce, but the chiles and garlic add a savory layer reminiscent of enchilada sauce. Use copious amounts for your fries, steak (yes, it works), or mix with *Smoked Garlic Aioli* (page 37) for an incredible burger sauce.

INGREDIENTS

2 pounds (900 g) tomatillos, washed and quartered
3 large dried guajillo chiles
1 garlic clove, peeled
1 cup (235 ml) distilled white vinegar
¼ cup (60 ml) water
½ cup (80 g) medium dice white onion
½ cup (115 g) brown sugar
½ teaspoon ground cloves
½ teaspoon ground allspice
1 teaspoon kosher salt

INSTRUCTIONS

Combine all ingredients in a large saucepan. Heat the pan on the stove over high heat, bringing it to a boil. Once the liquid starts to boil, reduce the heat to medium and cook for about 20 minutes. Stir often, as the tomatillos will release a lot of liquid.

Once everything has broken down, remove the pan from the heat. Pour all the contents into a large mesh strainer, draining any excess liquid. Transfer the drained contents into a blender and purée until smooth.

Pour the *Guajillo Ketchup* into a heatproof container and allow it to cool before you refrigerate. This will keep in the fridge for 3–4 weeks.

NOTE: It's crucial to drain the excess liquid in the strainer or your ketchup will be watery. The tangy flavors of tomatillos can vary, so adjust with additional brown sugar if it's too strong.

ARIZONA
ADOBO SAUCE

MAKES
ABOUT

2
CUPS
(480 G)

I'm here to tell you that I have a secret sauce in my pantry. This spicy paste is a cornerstone in our kitchen, the base ingredient for homemade chorizo, birria, and many different marinades. The combination of chiles and spices has changed throughout the years, evolving to my preferred tastes. The fruity ancho chile is the foundation, followed by the spicier guajillo. Adobo paste pairs so well with smoke and flames, just slather this on whatever meat you choose, marinate, and fire it up.

INGREDIENTS

5 dried ancho chiles, stemmed
    and seeded
4 dried guajillo chiles, stemmed
    and seeded
1 tablespoon (15 ml) canola oil
1 large white onion, chopped
8 garlic cloves, diced
2 tablespoons (14 g) smoked paprika
1 teaspoon black pepper
1 teaspoon dried Mexican oregano
1 teaspoon dried thyme
1 teaspoon ground cumin
½ teaspoon ground cinnamon
2 teaspoons kosher salt, plus more
    as needed
⅓ cup (80 ml) apple cider vinegar

INSTRUCTIONS

Clean the chiles with a damp paper towel. Heat a cast iron skillet on medium-high heat and toast the dried chiles, flipping occasionally, until puffed and lightly browned for 4–5 minutes. Place the chiles in a large bowl and pour hot water over them, allowing them to hydrate for about 20 minutes.

Turn the heat under the skillet to medium and add the oil. Once hot, add the onion and cook for 2–3 minutes until soft. Add the garlic and cook for another 2–3 minutes. Remove from the heat.

Add the chiles, sautéed onion, garlic, spices, and apple cider vinegar to a blender. Purée until you have a thick, paste-like sauce, using a splash of fresh water to help combine if needed. Taste and adjust with salt.

Use immediately or store in an airtight container in the fridge for 4–5 days or freeze for up to 3 months. The flavors will be better the next day after they have a chance to marinate.

SMOKY
SOUTHWEST HARISSA

MAKES ABOUT

2 CUPS

(512 G)

Harissa has exploded in popularity for the simple reason that it's an incredibly flavorful and versatile condiment. I'm always finding new ways to use this, and naturally, it fell into my food over the fire. Over time, I've created my own, using some authentic flavors from Tunisia as well as local chiles. Utilizing fresh chipotle chiles and roasted red bell pepper creates this smoky version that reminds me of a Mexican adobo. This recipe is used throughout the book to season salmon, shredded beef, and my personal favorite, *Harissa Habanero Butter* (page 122). Here's how I forge my version, ready to be stirred into anything.

INGREDIENTS

1 red bell pepper
6 dried guajillo chiles
2 dried chipotle morita chiles
1 tablespoon (6 g) cumin seeds
2 teaspoons coriander seeds
½ teaspoon fennel seeds
4 garlic cloves, minced
½ tablespoon smoked paprika
2 tablespoons (28 ml) fresh
    lemon juice
¼ cup (60 ml) olive oil
½ teaspoon sea salt, plus more
    as needed

INSTRUCTIONS

Preheat a grill or gas burner for high heat, 450–500°F (230–250°C). Char the red bell pepper on all sides until the skin has blackened and blistered, 5–7 minutes. Place the pepper into a sealed container, allowing it to steam as it cools. Remove and discard the skin, stem, and seeds.

Clean the chiles with a damp paper towel. Heat a cast iron skillet on medium-high heat and toast the dried chiles, flipping occasionally, until puffed and lightly browned for 4–5 minutes. Place the chiles in a large bowl and pour hot water over them, allowing them to hydrate for about 20 minutes.

Add the cumin, coriander, and fennel seeds to the hot skillet and shake for about 2 minutes, until the seeds become aromatic and slightly toasted.

Transfer all ingredients except the olive oil into a blender and purée until smooth. Stream in the olive oil at the end, blending until incorporated. Taste and adjust with salt if needed.

PICKLED
SWEET BELL PEPPERS

<table>
<tr><td>

MAKES ABOUT

3
CUPS
(600 G)

</td><td>

I came across pickled sweet bell peppers years ago at a beer-tasting event with a local brewery. They were sliced thin, served with a "barbecuterie" board alongside various condiments and meats. Working on my own recipe, I discover charring them first before pickling enhanced the sharp, sweet flavors of the bell peppers. Try them whole onto pulled beef sandwiches or even dicing them up fine into a relish. They are incredible when paired with spicy food, such as the *Gochujang Honey Mustard Chicken Sandwich* (page 109).

</td></tr>
</table>

INGREDIENTS

1 pound (455 g) whole sweet bell peppers, washed
1 tablespoon (15 ml) vegetable oil
1 cup (235 ml) water
1 cup (235 ml) distilled white vinegar
1 tablespoon (14 g) kosher salt
1 tablespoon (13 g) white sugar
4 garlic cloves
1 tablespoon (4 g) fresh dill
1 teaspoon black peppercorns

NOTE: Feel free to experiment with different combinations of aromatic spices and herbs. I love to use cumin seeds, Mexican oregano, and chile de árbol for a Southwest spin.

INSTRUCTIONS

Preheat the grill for direct cooking at medium-high heat, 350–400°F (180–200°C). Clean the grill grates and oil them as needed.

Toss the sweet bell peppers with the oil in a large bowl. Place the peppers on the hot grill and allow them to cook for a few minutes per side. The peppers should have some nice grill marks and start to soften. Be careful not to blacken the peppers. We are not trying to blister the skin. Remove them from the grill when ready.

In a medium pot, combine the water, vinegar, salt, and sugar and bring to a boil. Stir to dissolve the salt and sugar and then remove from the heat.

Place the peppers in a 1-quart (946 ml) Mason jar along with the garlic, dill, and peppercorns. Pour the brine over the peppers, making sure they are completely covered. Allow them to cool completely at room temperature before placing on the lid and putting into the refrigerator. They taste best if allowed to pickle for 24 hours and will keep in the fridge for up to 6 months.

PICKLED
JALAPEÑOS

MAKES ABOUT

3

CUPS
(720 G)

Open my fridge at any time and you'll see a jar of pickled jalapeños. We serve them alongside just about everything, providing that burst of acid and spice. Sure, they should be piled high on sandwiches or tacos, but they are also an amazing flavor booster when chopped up for sauces, dressings, or pastas.

INGREDIENTS

3 cups (270 g) jalapeño peppers, sliced into ⅛-inch (3 mm)-thick rings
1 tablespoon (14 g) kosher salt
1 cup (235 ml) water
1 cup (235 ml) distilled white vinegar
1 tablespoon (15 g) brown sugar
1 bay leaf
1 garlic clove, peeled
½ teaspoon dried Mexican oregano
½ teaspoon dried thyme

INSTRUCTIONS

In a medium pot, combine the water, vinegar, salt, brown sugar, bay leaf, garlic, oregano, and thyme and bring to a boil. Stir to dissolve the sugar and then remove from the heat.

Transfer the salted jalapeños to a 1-quart (946 ml) Mason jar or similar container. Pour the hot brine over the peppers and let the jar cool at room temperature until it can be handled. Cover with a secure lid and rest in the refrigerator for at least 8 hours. The jalapeños will stay good for up to 3–4 weeks, unless you eat them all first.

HOT PICKLED
RED ONIONS

MAKES ABOUT

3 CUPS

(672 G)

I was introduced to a variety of pickled red onions from the Yucatán called *Xnipec*, which means "dog snout." They're so spicy, your nose will sweat like a dog (*it happened*). Habanero peppers are generously mixed in with the red onions, adding substantial heat and fruity flavors to the condiment. Taking that inspiration home, these pickled red onions use a single habanero to add a moderate level of spice and flavor. Put these on tacos, sandwiches, or anything smoked. Make sure you have gloves handy when slicing this chile pepper!

INGREDIENTS
1 large red onion
1 habanero pepper
1 cup (235 ml) water
1 cup (235 ml) distilled white vinegar
1 tablespoon (13 g) white sugar
1 tablespoon (14 g) kosher salt
½ teaspoon dried Mexican oregano

INSTRUCTIONS
Slice the red onion in half and remove the skin. Slice the onion thinly using a mandoline or a knife.

Remove the stem and seeds from the habanero pepper. Cube the habanero using a brunoise cut: Slice the chile into long, thin strips and then rotate the strips 90 degrees and slice into small cubes.

In a medium pot, combine the water, vinegar, sugar, salt, and oregano and bring to a boil. Stir until the salt and sugar are dissolved.

Transfer the red onion and habanero to a 1-quart (946 ml) Mason jar or similar container. Pour the hot brine over the onion and cover the jar with plastic wrap. Let the jar cool at room temperature until it can be handled, cover with a secure lid, and rest in the refrigerator for at least 8 hours. The pickles will stay fresh for at least 2–3 weeks.

BRAZILIAN
VINAIGRETTE SALSA

Years ago, when I was at a Brazilian restaurant, this bright bowl of salsa was set on the table with slices of grilled bread. This amazing condiment is a cross between a salad dressing and a fresh pico de gallo salsa. Tasting some with my steak shocked me—my taste buds came alive with the vibrant flavors of tomatoes, peppers, and herbs. Salt and acid from the vinaigrette seasoned the steak, enhancing that big beefy flavor I crave. This is a mild salsa, given there are no spicy chiles involved. It's quick to prepare and makes a generous portion for a crowd. If you're like me and struggle with salsa self-control, it might serve fewer.

INGREDIENTS

2 large ripe tomatoes

1 small white onion

1 green bell pepper

1 yellow bell pepper

½ cup (120 ml) olive oil

½ cup (120 ml) distilled white vinegar

5 tablespoons (20 g) fresh parsley, chopped

1 tablespoon (3 g) dried Mexican oregano, crushed

½ teaspoon fresh ground black pepper

½ teaspoon salt, plus more as needed

INSTRUCTIONS

Halve the tomatoes and scoop out the seeds. Dice the tomatoes into small pieces, about ¼ inch (6 mm). Dice the onion and bell peppers to the same size, keeping them uniform.

In a small bowl, combine the olive oil and vinegar, whisking briefly to mix them. Add the diced vegetables, parsley, oregano, pepper, and salt to taste. Allow the vinaigrette to rest in the fridge, covered, for at least an hour before serving. This salsa will stay fresh for up to 2 days due to the high level of acidity.

CHARRED POBLANO
PICO DE GALLO

MAKES ABOUT
2
CUPS
(480 G)

Pico de gallo is known for fresh preparation and crisp textures, bringing a bright flavor to anything from chips to tacos. This recipe swaps out the classic jalapeño for a combination of poblanos and serrano chiles, both prepared in a way that highlights their strengths. Charring the poblanos enhances their sweetness and tames the grassy, bitter flavors. Crisp serrano chiles step in with a sharp heat, making up for the mild spice of the poblanos. The only problem with this salsa is that by the time I need it for tacos, half of it is missing, along with most of our tortilla chips.

INGREDIENTS
2 poblano chiles
4 Roma tomatoes, seeded and diced
1 serrano chile, minced
½ medium red onion, diced
¼ cup (4 g) chopped fresh cilantro
Juice of 1 lime
Salt and black pepper

INSTRUCTIONS
Preheat the grill for direct cooking at high heat, 450–500°F (230–250°C). Clean the grill grates and oil them as needed.

Place the poblano chiles on the grill and char each side until the skin is dark and blistered all over. Remove from the grill and place in a sealed container for about 10 minutes while the steam releases the skin. Remove and discard the skin, seeds, and stem.

Dice the poblano and add it to a bowl along with the tomatoes, serrano chile, red onion, and cilantro. Squeeze in the lime juice and season with salt and pepper to taste. Stir. This will stay fresh in the fridge for 3–5 days.

NOTE: The poblanos can also be charred in an oven with the broiler for about 5 minutes, rotating as needed to char each side. Swap out the serrano for jalapeños for a milder heat. A sweeter option would be to roast red bell peppers in place of the poblanos.

BRISKET, BURGERS, BEEF & LAMB

CHILES AND SMOKE
BURGER

MAKES
4
BURGERS

One of the most memorable burgers I've ever had was from a neighborhood bar called the *Windsor*. Their house burger has these incredibly rich, sweet, caramelized onions piled neatly on a slice of melted sharp cheddar. Those complex yet simple flavors inspired my signature *Chiles and Smoke Burger*. This burger takes some time to prepare, but the condiments can all be made ahead of time. Caramelized onions and jalapeños garnish the peppery beef, which sits upon crispy charred cabbage. The burger sauce smeared onto the toasted buns is a fusion of the *Guajillo Ketchup* and *Smoked Garlic Aioli*, reminding you that this burger has some bite.

CARAMELIZED ONIONS AND JALAPEÑOS

2 jalapeño peppers
1½ tablespoons (25 ml) olive oil
4 large white onions, cut into thin slices
1 teaspoon kosher salt

GRILLED BURGER

1½ pounds (680 g) ground chuck or brisket (80/20 preferred)
Kosher salt and fresh ground black pepper
4 brioche burger buns, halved

CHARRED CABBAGE

½ medium-sized head cabbage
1½ tablespoons (25 ml) olive oil
Kosher salt

GUAJILLO BURGER SAUCE

2 tablespoons (30 g) *Guajillo Ketchup* (page 39)

¼ cup (60 g) *Smoked Garlic Aioli* (page 37)
1 tablespoon (9 g) chopped pickles
½ teaspoon apple cider vinegar

INSTRUCTIONS

Prepare the caramelized onions and jalapeño peppers. Slice the jalapeños in half along the length. Remove the seeds and membrane for a mild heat. Slice the jalapeños into thin slices. Coat the bottom of a wide stainless pan with the olive oil, heating the pan on medium-high heat until the oil is shimmering. Add the onion and jalapeño slices and stir to coat with the oil. Sprinkle with some salt and spread the vegetables out evenly over the pan, stirring very occasionally.

Cook for 30 minutes, lower the heat slightly, and continue to let the onions and jalapeños cook. They will start to stick to the bottom of the pan after 45–60 minutes. Scrape them with a metal spatula, continuing to cook until they are a rich, browned color. Add a splash of water as needed, continuing to cook for up to 2 hours or until desired.

Prepare the grill for a 2-zone cooking setup at medium-high heat, 350–400°F (180–200°C), with the hot coals on one side. Clean the grill grates and oil them as needed.

Divide the beef into four even portions. Form the potions into patties and place them onto a sheet tray or plate and into the fridge until ready. ➤➤

Slice the cabbage half into 6 slices, keeping the core intact. Lightly rub the olive oil onto the face of the cabbage. Place the cabbage cut-side down on the grill and sear until charred for 5–6 minutes. Flip over and char the second side. Remove the cabbage when completely seared and set aside until it's cool enough to handle. Slice off the core and discard. Thinly slice the cabbage and lightly salt to taste.

It's time to cook the burgers. Pull the tray out of the fridge and season the top of the burgers with salt and pepper. Place them facedown on the grill, directly over the coals. Close the lid of the grill and sear for 3–4 minutes to develop a nice crust. Remove the lid and carefully flip the burgers to a clean spot on the grill, still over the coals. If the burgers are cooking too quickly, move them to the cooler side of the grill to finish. They should be done within a few more minutes, with an internal temperature of about 160°F (71°C). Remove the burgers and allow them to rest for a few minutes.

In a small bowl, mix the *Guajillo Ketchup*, *Smoked Garlic Aioli*, pickles, and apple cider vinegar together for the burger sauce. Toast the buns on the grill briefly.

Spread the *Guajillo Burger Sauce* on the bottom bun. Top with some *Charred Cabbage*, the burger, and the *Caramelized Onions and Jalapeños*. Take a crispy, juicy bite and enjoy.

GOCHUJANG
CHILI CON CARNE

Sampling different recipes at an office chili cook-off years ago, I became incredibly jealous: I didn't have my own signature chili. Shouldn't every backyard griller? Any recipe wouldn't do. My bowl was going to be complex, savory, spicy, and prepared without using any powdered chiles. After years of tweaking, I finally have my perfect recipe. Fresh jalapeño and smoky chipotles were chosen for the foundation, the addition of savory gochujang tying everything together. Seared beef is gently tenderized for hours, swimming in dark beer, beef broth, and fire-roasted tomatoes. The sharp heat from the jalapeños and chipotles sears the tongue, while the gochujang adds a warmth in the throat. My only advice is to double the recipe if you want to eat any the next day. Everyone will be having seconds.

INGREDIENTS

4 tablespoons (60 ml) vegetable oil

1½ pounds (680 g) chuck roast, cut into ½-inch (1.3 cm) cubes

1 teaspoon kosher salt

1 teaspoon black pepper

1 jalapeño pepper, finely diced

1 red onion, finely diced

3 garlic cloves, finely diced

1 chipotle chile in adobo sauce, finely diced

2 teaspoons adobo sauce from the chipotle chiles

1 tablespoon (7 g) ground cumin

1 teaspoon ground coriander

1 tablespoon (15 g) dark brown sugar

5 tablespoons (75 g) gochujang

2 cups (475 ml) beef broth

1 cup (235 ml) Negra Modelo, or preferred dark beer

1 can (15 ounces, or 425 g) fire-roasted tomatoes

½ cup (8 g) chopped fresh cilantro

INSTRUCTIONS

Preheat the grill at medium-high heat, 350–400°F (180–200°C). We'll be searing meat in a Dutch oven or deep cast iron pot.

Place the Dutch oven on the grates above the coals. Add 2 tablespoons (30 ml) of the oil to the pot, warming it until it shimmers. While the oil is heating up, lightly season the meat with salt and pepper on all sides. Add some of the meat to the pot, allowing it to sear. Flip as needed to create a crispy crust on each side. You'll probably need to do this in batches; otherwise, the pot will be too crowded. Once browned, transfer the seared beef to a plate lined with a paper towel. ➼

NOTE: Put the lid on while cooking if you like the chili to have a thinner consistency and simmer without the lid if you like it a little thicker.

Adjust the coals or temperature of the grill to medium heat, 300–350°F (150–180°C). Add the remaining 2 tablespoons (30 ml) of oil into the pot. Once the oil is hot, add the jalapeño pepper and red onion. Stir frequently for about 2 minutes until the onion has softened. Add the garlic, chipotle chile, adobo sauce, cumin, coriander, and brown sugar. Continue to stir to incorporate all of the aromatics and spices.

In a medium-size bowl, whisk together the gochujang and beef broth. Add this into the pot along with the beer and fire-roasted tomatoes with juices. I recommend using a wooden spoon to scrape up the bits on the bottom of the pot. Add the meat back to the pot and bring it all to a simmer. Place the lid on the pot to cover it.

Check every hour and stir gently, checking to make sure the meat is tender. This should take 2–3 hours depending on your heat source.

Stir in the chopped cilantro at the end. I recommend serving with white rice, shredded cheddar cheese, and other fun toppings. I've been known to pack this into a large flour tortilla—you really can't go wrong.

SMOKED
SONORAN CHILI

SERVES
ABOUT
8
PEOPLE

I'm not going to try to convince you to take a stance on beans with chili, so don't worry. This delicious and smoky recipe has evolved so much over time, originating back to eating at the kitchen table with my parents when I was a child. My family is from Michigan, so stews and chilis were part of the regular rounds. Living in Arizona and having exposure to the local culture influenced the flavors over time, growing spicier and bolder. Smoking the chili during the simmering phase allows the flavors to develop slowly, while adding that extra bath of wood-fire essence to permeate. You can customize the heat and layers of flavor by using either the *Light Chili Powder* or *Spicy Chili Powder*.

INGREDIENTS

4 cups (946 ml) beef broth

2 cups (475 ml) water

2 pounds (900 g) lean ground beef, 90/10 preferred

1 large onion, minced (about 3 cups [480 g])

3 jalapeño peppers, diced

6 garlic cloves, minced

1 can (16 ounces, or 455 g) tomato sauce

¼ cup (32 g) *Light Chili Powder* or *Spicy Chili Powder* (page 31)

1 teaspoon ground cumin

1 teaspoon ground cinnamon

½ teaspoon ground allspice

¼ teaspoon ground cloves

2 teaspoons kosher salt

2 tablespoons (28 ml) Worcestershire sauce

1 tablespoon (15 ml) apple cider vinegar

1 ounce (28 g) unsweetened chocolate

FOR SERVING

1 small white onion, finely diced (optional)

8 ounces (225 g) sharp cheddar cheese, grated (optional)

Charred Poblano Pico de Gallo (page 53; optional)

Sour cream (optional)

INSTRUCTIONS

Put the beef broth and water into a Dutch oven and heat it to a low boil. Add the ground beef a little at a time until it separates into small pieces. Stir and break it up with a fork to a fine texture and turn the stove down to a low simmer for 30 minutes.

While the beef simmers, preheat the smoker to 250°F (120°C).

Add the rest of the ingredients to the Dutch oven, stirring to incorporate, and simmer for 10 minutes. Transfer the uncovered pot to the smoker and cook for 3–4 hours, stirring every 30 minutes. Taste and adjust.

Chili has a reputation for developing flavors overnight in the fridge. Let it cool and transfer to the fridge. The next day, skim any excess fat off the top and reheat the chili on low heat on the stove or grill. Serve a warm bowl of chili with chopped white onion and cheddar or even *Charred Poblano Pico de Gallo* (page 53) with sour cream.

NOTE: This recipe can easily be made over the stove or in the oven, but stirring occasionally in the smoker adds a nice depth of flavor that can't be reproduced. Make sure you leave the lid off so the chili can absorb the smoke.

SONORAN
"RED HOTS"

MAKES

8

CHILI
DOGS

I've consumed a lot of hot dogs in my lifetime, no regrets. My Midwest family introduced me to Coney dogs and Michigan Red Hots, a regional all-beef hot dog topped with a meaty chili, onions, and yellow mustard. Growing up, we almost always served a type of chili with hot dogs at the kitchen table. These days, I steer toward a delicious regional treat in Arizona. We have Sonoran dogs, these grilled bacon-wrapped hot dogs, topped with a cluster of fresh toppings such as pico de gallo, guacamole, crema, and much more. Fusing my love for the Midwest and local flavors, an all-beef hotdog is wrapped in bacon and smoked alongside the pot of *Smoked Sonoran Chili*. This rich and spicy dog is topped with sour cream and *Charred Poblano Pico de Gallo* to balance the flavors. Grab a pile of napkins and get ready.

INGREDIENTS

8 beef hot dogs
8 strips bacon
8 hot dog buns
3–4 cups (708–944 g)
 Smoked Sonoran Chili
 (page 62; warmed)

FOR SERVING

Sour cream
Charred Poblano Pico de Gallo
 (page 53)

INSTRUCTIONS

Wrap each hot dog with a single piece of bacon. Use a toothpick to hold it in place if needed or carefully set them seam-side down. Placing them in the fridge for a few hours ahead of time will help adhere the bacon.

To smoke: Preheat the smoker to 250°F (120°C). Place the hot dogs on the grill, seam-side down, and smoke for 2–3 hours. The bacon will be mostly rendered down and smoked after 2 hours, but that last hour helps to crisp it up even more.

To grill: Preheat the grill for direct cooking at medium-high heat, 350–400°F (180–200°C). Clean the grill grates and oil them as needed. Place the hot dogs directly over the coals carefully and rotate frequently. Cook for 6–8 minutes total, making sure all sides are lightly crisp to your preference. Toothpicks are definitely recommended if you're planning to grill.

Assemble the chili dogs. Place a bacon-wrapped hot dog into a bun, and cover with a generous portion of warm *Smoked Sonoran Chili*. Top with sour cream and *Charred Poblano Pico de Gallo* and enjoy.

NOTE: Add these bacon-wrapped hot dogs into the smoker while your *Smoked Sonoran Chili* is cooking. I like to utilize the real estate of a smoker as much as possible, and there's practically no additional effort needed. To amp up the heat, sprinkle a portion of the *Light Chili Powder* (page 31) to the outside of the bacon before cooking. There's very little salt, but lots of additional flavor you'd be adding.

SMOKED HARISSA
BEEF TACOS

SERVES

4–6

PEOPLE

The first time I cooked it, the warm and spicy flavors of this juicy, shredded beef left me speechless . . . and I hadn't even made tacos out of it yet. Inspired by flavors from Africa, the beef is slowly smoked for hours before taking a steam bath with salty beef broth and pungent harissa paste. The tacos are served with a dice of fresh red onion and tomato, brightening the rich flavors from the beef and salsa. Flour tortillas are recommended, as the juicy beef and salsa will be soaked up. Nothing should be left behind.

HARISSA BEEF

1½ tablespoons (21 g) kosher salt
1 tablespoon (7 g) smoked paprika
1 teaspoon black pepper
½ teaspoon garlic powder
¼ teaspoon ground cinnamon
1 beef chuck roast, 3–4 pounds
    (1.4–1.8 kg)
1¼ cups (295 ml) beef broth
¾ cup (192 g) *Smoky Southwest
    Harissa* (page 42)

SALSA

2 Roma tomatoes, seeded and diced
½ medium red onion, diced
¼ cup (4 g) chopped fresh cilantro
Juice of 1 lime
Salt and black pepper

TACOS

12 flour tortillas, preferably small
1 cup (145 g) roasted peanuts, crushed

INSTRUCTIONS

Mix the kosher salt, paprika, pepper, garlic powder, and cinnamon together in a small bowl. Season the chuck roast on all sides with the spice mixture and allow it to rest at room temperature while the smoker warms up.

Prepare the smoker for indirect cooking at 250°F (120°C). This process will take roughly 6–7 hours, so make sure to plan accordingly.

Place the chuck roast in the smoker and allow it to cook for 3–4 hours until the internal temperature reaches 165°F (74°C).

Warm up the beef broth over low heat and whisk in the *Smoky Southwest Harissa*. Once the beef reaches the target temperature, place it into a Dutch oven or skillet with a lid. Pour the broth and harissa mixture over the beef. Place the lid on the pot and place it back into the smoker, increasing the temperature to 285°F (141°C).

Allow the beef to continue to cook for another 2–3 hours until the internal temperature is about 205°F (96°C). The temperature probe should poke right through the beef, and it should feel like smooth peanut butter. Remove the pot from the smoker and allow it to rest, with the lid on, for about 30 minutes. Once the meat has rested, go ahead and

shred it sitting in the juices. I recommend using gloves and getting in with your hands. This is the easiest way.

Prepare the salsa. Mix the tomatoes, red onion, cilantro, and lime juice in a small bowl and season with salt and pepper to taste.

Warm up the flour tortillas and serve. Add the shredded beef, the salsa, and top with the crushed peanuts.

COFFEE-RUBBED TRI-TIP
WITH SHISHITO GREMOLATA

<table>
<tr><td>

SERVES

4–6

PEOPLE

</td></tr>
</table>

Grilled shishito peppers can certainly hold their own on a menu, but they are also incredible paired with bright flavors. Here, they are chopped up and mixed with rich walnuts, fresh lemon, and herbs to create a complex and vibrant topping for the most incredible steak. I love to use tri-tip, which gets a crispy crust on the outside while maintaining a tender, juicy interior. This tri-tip is seasoned with *Smoky Coffee Rub* and cooked slowly with smoke until it's ready to be seared. The dark coffee crust is bitter and earthy, complementing the grassy notes of the shishitos and parsley. The fatty flavors from the gremolata pair well with tri-tip, being a leaner cut than most other steaks.

TRI-TIP
1 tri-tip steak, 2–3 pounds
  (900 g–1.4 kg)
4 tablespoons (28 g) *Smoky
  Coffee Rub* (page 33)

SHISHITO GREMOLATA
20 shishito peppers
½ cup (30 g) chopped fresh parsley
1 garlic clove, chopped
½ teaspoon lemon zest
3 tablespoons (45 ml) fresh
  lemon juice
1 tablespoon (10 g) chopped shallot
½ cup (60 g) chopped walnuts
3 tablespoons (45 ml) olive oil
Salt and black pepper

EQUIPMENT
Grilling skewers (metal or wooden)

INSTRUCTIONS

Trim the tri-tip to clean it up of any silver skin or trimmings. Generously season with the *Smoky Coffee Rub* and set aside to rest while you heat up the grill.

Prepare the grill for a 2-zone cooking setup at 250–275°F (120–140°C), with the hot coals on one side. Optionally, add some hardwood for smoke flavor, such as oak.

Set the tri-tip on the cooler side of the grill away from the coals. Check the steak during this time, flipping as needed to ensure even cooking. For medium-rare, cook the steak during this phase until 115–120°F (46–49°C). Allow it to slowly cook for 45–60 minutes, until the internal temperature is 15–20 degrees from your target temperature.

Remove the steak when it reaches temperature. Adjust the hot side of the grill to make sure it's ready for direct searing. Open the vents if you need to. Aim for 400–450°F (200–230°C). Clean the grill grates and oil them as needed. ➤➤

> **NOTE:** If you're using wooden skewers, soak them in water for at least 30 minutes in advance to prevent them from burning when cooking on the grill.

Thread the shishito peppers on the skewers for direct grilling. Place them over the coals until charred on the first side, about 2 minutes. Flip and repeat. Once they are blistered and charred, remove them from the grill and let them cool for a few minutes while the steak sears.

Place the tri-tip directly over the coals and sear for 2 minutes, flipping to repeat. Continue to sear and flip, creating a crust while allowing the hot side to cool. This will control the momentum of the heat on the surface, allowing for a proper sear and minimizing the formation of a gray band developing inside the steak between the exterior and the interior. Remove the steak after a few flips when it reaches your target temperature, 130–135°F (54–57°C) for medium-rare. Allow it to rest and prepare the gremolata.

Remove the stems of the shishitos if you haven't and chop the peppers. Place them in a bowl with the parsley, garlic, lemon zest, lemon juice, shallot, walnuts, and olive oil. Mix well, adding salt and pepper to taste.

Slice the steak against the grain and serve with the *Shishito Gremolata*.

REVERSE-SEARING

The process used to cook this steak is called "reverse-searing," coming from the concept of slowly cooking meat at a low temperature before the searing process. It's generally used for thick steaks and roasts, providing an edge-to-edge pink center with a crispy crust on the outside. You can accomplish this using a smoker, grill, or even the oven using temperatures between 225–275°F (107–140°C). The main key is making sure that the meat is pulled out of the initial cooking 15–20 degrees before your preferred target temperature. This allows you to sear at a high heat quickly without overcooking, eliminating those unappetizing thick, gray bands encircling the meat!

FIRECRACKER
BRISKET

SERVES

12–14

PEOPLE

There are different schools of thought when it comes to brisket. Some people only use salt and pepper to create the bark. I'm a fan of that method, but I also think brisket shouldn't have rules. Over a number of years, I have experimented with many combinations, eventually landing on a spicy blend of chiles, peppercorns, and aromatics that makes a truly impressive bark. The first bite explodes in your mouth, picking up notes of sharp pepper, flowery pops of fennel and Szechuan peppercorns, and the sweet heat of Korean chile flakes. Maybe that's why one of my friends came up with the name "Firecracker" for this recipe. Don't worry: The taste of perfectly smoked beef still shines through.

1 whole packer brisket, 12–14 pounds
(5.5–6.4 kg)

FIRECRACKER BRISKET RUB
2 tablespoons (20 g) black
peppercorns
1 tablespoon (3 g) Szechuan
peppercorns
1 tablespoon (6 g) fennel seeds
1 teaspoon whole yellow mustard
seeds
3 tablespoons (48 g) gochugaru flakes
3 tablespoons (42 g) kosher salt
1 tablespoon (13 g) white sugar
1 teaspoon garlic powder

SPRITZ
Apple cider vinegar

EQUIPMENT
Spray bottle
Pink butcher paper

INSTRUCTIONS

Trim the brisket and keep any scraps (we're going to use them). Using a boning knife, slice off a slender edge around the outside edges, about ¼ inch (3 mm) thick. Depending on how thin the flat of your brisket is, slice off the thin edges, rounding out the front of it. Trim the point sticking up, clean up the shape, and remove any thin areas of meat or fat.

Place the brisket on your board with the fat side up. Carefully trim the excess fat, leaving about ¼ inch (6 mm) behind. There's a hard lump of fat on the top near the point, cut out most of that, again leaving about ¼ inch (6 mm) behind. You'll notice there is a thick pocket of fat in the seam just below the point muscle. Clean up the outside of it but leave it there for the cooking process. This can be removed when slicing. ➤➤

Flip your brisket so the fat side is facing down. Trim all silver skin and excess pieces of fat on the lean side. Remove the fat on the underside of the brisket point.

Prepare the rub. Preheat a small pan on medium heat. Toast the black peppercorns, Szechuan peppercorns, and fennel seeds for a few minutes until aromatic and remove to cool. Grind the peppercorns, fennel, and mustard seeds in a spice grinder for a medium-coarse blend. Add to a small bowl and mix in the gochugaru, salt, sugar, and garlic powder until well combined.

Season the brisket generously on all sides with the *Firecracker Brisket Rub*. You can do this hours ahead of time, even a day before. Place the brisket on a wire rack in the fridge, uncovered, until ready to use.

Trim the scraps for smoked beef tallow. Slice the pieces of fat into roughly 1-inch (2.5 cm) pieces, discarding the meat (you can reserve for grinding if you'd like). When ready to smoke the brisket, place the fat with ¼ cup (60 ml) water in a grill-safe pan with a lid.

Preheat the smoker to 250°F (120°C). Take the brisket out of the fridge and set it on the counter for about an hour to come up closer to room temperature. Place the brisket in your smoker with the point closest to the heat source. I recommend fat-side down, which helps to keep the seasoning on the meat and also looks better when slicing. If you're using a pellet smoker, pay attention to where the firepot is located underneath the deflector shield. Place the grill-safe pan with beef trimmings in the smoker. Shut the lid and leave the brisket to cook for 3 hours, undisturbed.

When you open the smoker, check the brisket trimmings. They should have mostly rendered down, forming a pool of melted brisket fat with crispy bits. You may continue to render these down longer if needed or strain the liquid into a jar with a cheesecloth or fine-mesh strainer.

Spritz the edges of your brisket with vinegar to prevent them from drying out. Shut the smoker and continue to cook, opening it every 45 minutes to spritz until the brisket hits about 165°F (74°C) internal temperature. This temperature is a milestone during the cooking phase as the brisket will start to stall, the moisture is exiting the brisket so rapidly that the temperature will not rise for a long time without some assistance.

So, let's help it out to get past the stall: Set your brisket onto a very large sheet of pink butcher paper, it will be rolled up tight with 2 layers. Take about ¼ cup (60 ml) of the beef tallow that you rendered and pour a light, even layer across the top of the brisket. Roll the brisket in the paper, tucking in the sides after the first roll. Make sure you pay attention to which side is the top and place it back onto the smoker, with the top facing up. Turn up the heat in the smoker to 265–275°F (129–140°C) and continue to cook the brisket until it reaches about 200°F (93°C) internal temperature.

> **NOTE:** Check for tenderness with your temp probe on the flat, the middle, and the point. If the brisket feels jiggly or flexible overall, it's done. Still, allow it to rest for **at least 2 hours** at room temperature, still in the butcher paper, tented with some aluminum foil.
>
> Slice the brisket when you are ready to serve, not before. Use a long, sharp blade without serration. Slice the flat against the grain. The point muscle should be sliced in half lengthwise.

MORE REST
IS BEST

THE BRISKET IN THE SMOKER spends a long time working hard, forcing out excess moisture and rendering fat. Just like anyone after a workout, it needs a proper cooldown period. Resting a brisket is a process that allows it to cool very slowly over time, relaxing the constricted muscles. The moment the brisket comes out of the smoker, the juices inside are closer toward the surface, ready to spill out once the meat is cut. Given enough time to cool off, those juices will redistribute throughout the meat, as the fibers are no longer contracting. Allow the brisket to rest as long as possible, for a minimum of 2 hours, keeping it above 145°F (63°C) internal temperature. The easiest way to accomplish this is to leave the brisket fully wrapped in the butcher paper and cover it with loosely tented foil.

Some people immediately wrap the hot brisket coming off the smoker in foil, then a towel, and place it in a cooler to rest for hours. However, I've found insulating the brisket using this method before allowing it to switch to a "cool-down mode" can continue to cook it, forcing out more of the moisture. Do that, and when it's time to eat, the brisket will likely be sitting in a pool of all the juices that were meant to be inside the meat.

SKIRT STEAK TACOS

Skirt steak is the best for soaking up flavorful marinades, especially this *Spicy Garlic Mojo Sauce*. Every bite from these tacos is incredibly rich, from the charred beef to the *Creamy Corn Salsa*. Cook the steak with a high heat, which allows you to quickly build a crispy crust on the outside without overcooking the middle. I recommend cooking to a medium temperature, due to the coarse grain and high fat content. Tacos are my preferred transportation to mouth, but this meal also works well served over rice or just right off the cutting board.

SPICY GARLIC MOJO SAUCE

20 garlic cloves, peeled
1 cup (235 ml) olive oil
¼ cup (4 g) fresh cilantro, leaves
  and stems
2 tablespoons (30 g) chipotle chiles in
  adobo sauce, plus more as needed
½ teaspoon kosher salt, plus more
  as needed
½ teaspoon black pepper
½ teaspoon dried Mexican oregano
Juice of 2 limes

SKIRT STEAK

2–3 pounds (900 g –1.4 kg) skirt steak
1 teaspoon kosher salt
¾ cup (188 g) *Spicy Garlic Mojo Sauce*

CREAMY CORN SALSA

4 ears sweet corn, husked
¾ cup (180 g) Mexican crema
  (or sour cream)
1 jalapeño pepper, seeded,
  diced finely

½ cup (8 g) chopped fresh cilantro
½ medium white onion, diced
Juice of 1 lime
1–2 teaspoons *Spicy Chili Powder* (page 31)
Kosher salt

FOR SERVING

8–10 corn tortillas
Hot Pickled Red Onions (page 48)
Slices of lime

INSTRUCTIONS

Prepare the mojo sauce first by preheating the oven to 300°F (150°C, or gas mark 2). This can be prepared days ahead of time.

Place the garlic cloves into a medium, ovenproof saucepan. Pour in the olive oil, making sure that the garlic is covered. Cover the pot with aluminum foil or a lid and place it in the oven. Cook for about 45 minutes. Garlic aromas will be coming out of the oven, and the cloves should

start to be a golden, nutty brown in appearance. The texture will be soft, almost like peanut butter.

Remove the pot from the oven and let the garlic and oil cool completely to room temperature. Place the garlic, oil, ➤

cilantro, chipotle chiles, salt, pepper, and oregano in a blender. Purée until the mix is very smooth and squeeze in the lime juice. Blend briefly to mix, season, and adjust if needed. This should have a strong, spicy, and salty flavor.

Slice the skirt steak into 2 manageable pieces, making sure they will fit on your grill. Pat the steaks dry and season with the salt on each side. Brush the *Spicy Garlic Mojo Sauce* on each side and place the steak in a resealable container. Allow the steak to marinate in the fridge for at least 2 hours, up to overnight.

Preheat the grill for direct cooking at medium-high heat, 350–400°F (180–200°C). Clean the grill grates and oil them as needed.

Grill the corn first, cooking for 8–10 minutes total with the lid closed. Turn the corn every few minutes to cook evenly and build char. Remove the corn from the grill when ready and allow to cool.

Turn up the heat a little and place the skirt steaks on the grill. The oils from the marinade may drip down into the coals, so be mindful. Flip the steaks every minute or so for 6–8 minutes total. Aim for about 130°F (54°C) internal temperature if you're cooking to a medium finish and remove the steaks from the grill. Allow them to rest and prepare the salsa.

Cut off the corn kernels and add them to a bowl. Mix the other salsa ingredients with the corn, adding as much *Spicy Chili Powder* as you'd like for additional heat. Season with salt to taste.

Slice the steak into cubes. Trust me, you don't want to take a bite and have all of the filling slide out. Serve with warm corn tortillas, *Creamy Corn Salsa*, *Hot Pickled Red Onions*, and slices of lime.

PLANKED JALAPEÑO
MEAT LOAF
WITH GUAJILLO BOURBON GLAZE

Cooking with bourbon is just fun—let's admit it. Plus, it's a pleasure to enjoy with pretty much all types of grilled and smoked meats. The sweet, smoky alcohol adds a rich complexity to this *Jalapeño Meat Loaf* and happens to naturally tenderize the beef by breaking down enzymes. Smoking a meat loaf can be physically tricky, but using a wooden plank provides a perfect surface for it to rest on while adding a flavorful moisture barrier. The *Guajillo Ketchup*, combined with bourbon, creates a tangy, sweet glaze, complementing the rich flavors of the beef. Slice and serve right off the plank.

JALAPEÑO MEAT LOAF

2 jalapeño peppers

2 pounds (900 g) ground beef, 90/10 fat ratio

1 cup (63 g) finely crushed tortilla chips

1 cup (160 g) grated white onion

½ cup (8 g) fresh cilantro, finely chopped

2 garlic cloves, minced

1 teaspoon guajillo chile powder

1 teaspoon smoked paprika

1 teaspoon kosher salt

½ teaspoon black pepper

1 teaspoon Worcestershire sauce

1 tablespoon (15 ml) bourbon

2 large eggs, beaten

GUAJILLO BOURBON GLAZE

½ cup (120 g) *Guajillo Ketchup* (page 39)

2 tablespoons (30 g) brown sugar

1 tablespoon (15 ml) bourbon

EQUIPMENT

1 Cedar grilling plank, about 5 x 11 inches (13 x 28 cm)

INSTRUCTIONS

Preheat the grill or gas burner to char the jalapeño peppers. Grill them until the skin blisters and chars and place them in a plastic bag or sealed container to steam and soften for a few minutes. Peel off the skins and discard the stems and seeds. Chop the jalapeños into a fine dice.

Transfer the ground beef and remaining meat loaf ingredients into a large bowl, including the jalapeños. Mix well with your hands, making sure everything is evenly distributed. Test the meat mixture by searing a small amount in a pan until it is cooked through. Adjust the seasonings if needed and allow the meat to rest in the fridge for about 30 minutes before forming into shape.

Pour warm water over the cedar grilling plank, allowing it to soak for 20–30 minutes while the meat is in the fridge. Make sure the wood is submerged in a container or baking tray by placing a weight on it.

Prepare the smoker for indirect cooking at 350°F (180°C).

Remove the wood plank from the water and wipe it clean. Form the meat mixture into a loaf shape on the cedar plank. Transfer your planked meat loaf into the smoker and close the lid. Allow it to cook for 1 hour undisturbed.

Prepare the glaze by mixing the ingredients together in a small saucepan on low heat for a few minutes. The brown sugar will melt, and the mixture will thicken slightly. Use this to glaze the meat loaf when the internal temperature is about 145°F (63°C). Brush all sides of the meat loaf and continue to cook.

Remove the meat loaf when it reaches 160°F (71°C) and allow it to rest for about 10 minutes before carving. Serve with a glass of your favorite bourbon and enjoy.

NOTE: Use a lower-proof bourbon that you enjoy. The smoky, sweet profile will be more prominent in the meat loaf, and you'll avoid strong alcohol flavors.

SHISHITO
CHEESESTEAK QUESO

MAKES ABOUT

5
CUPS
(1.4 KG)

Years ago, I had the idea to make sandwiches with thinly-sliced smoked brisket and grilled shishito peppers, slathered with a creamy cheese sauce. Over time, the sandwiches turned into a party dish, incorporating more classic cheesesteak ingredients with shaved ribeye, onions, and peppers. Still, the nontraditional goat cheese and shishitos are the key ingredients in this skillet—the grassy, bitter flavors of the shishito pair perfectly with the sweet, tangy bite of goat cheese. Grill up some thin slices of bread while you have the charcoal going. It's the perfect vehicle for transferring this dip to your mouth.

1 tablespoon (15 ml) canola oil

1 small sweet onion, diced

½ red bell pepper, diced

½ cup (45 g) diced shishito peppers

1 ribeye steak (14 ounces, or 390 g), shaved

½ teaspoon kosher salt

½ teaspoon black pepper

GOAT CHEESE QUESO

1½ cups (355 g) half-and-half

8 ounces (225 g) goat cheese, at room temperature

16 ounces (455 g) Velveeta Queso Blanco, cubed

1 cup (115 g) finely grated Monterey Jack cheese

1 cup (115 g) finely grated cheddar cheese

Salt

INSTRUCTIONS

Preheat the grill for direct cooking at medium heat, 300–350°F (150–180°C).

Heat up the oil in a 12-inch (30 cm) cast iron skillet on the grill. Add the onion, red bell pepper, and shishito peppers, stirring occasionally as they cook. The peppers and onion will start to brown and caramelize after 15–20 minutes. Transfer them to a dish and set aside.

Add the steak to the skillet and cook, stirring frequently. Season with the salt and pepper while cooking and stirring. After about 5 minutes, the steak should be seared and ready to be removed and added to the dish with the peppers and onion.

Carefully wipe out the excess oil in the skillet. Pour in the half-and-half and allow it to warm up completely, just before it starts to simmer. Break the goat cheese into small pieces, adding a little at a time while whisking to mix. This step is much easier if the goat cheese is already at room temperature. Add the Velveeta next, continuing to whisk and melt. Slowly add the Monterey Jack and cheddar until everything is mixed and melted. Taste and season with salt as needed, being mindful that the beef is already salted.

Stir in the steak and peppers and onion and warm them up together for a few minutes before serving.

BIG BEEF RIBS
WITH BARBACOA SAUCE

SERVES
4–5
PEOPLE

Everyone stops to stare when big beef ribs are sliced open. The blade crushes through the crusty bark, revealing a scarlet ring surrounding impossibly juicy beef. Each bite is incredibly rich, packed with flavors of the smoke and spices. This is a special dish, not your everyday barbecue. I'm inspired by traditional barbacoa, the earthy flavors of chiles, herbs, and spices slowly cooked with meat over the open fire. Barbacoa has evolved over time, more commonly prepared in a steamy environment rather than slowly smoked. Drawing from both methods of cooking, these beef ribs present themselves with a smoky, crispy bark served with a roasted barbacoa sauce. Bright chiles are fortified with beef stock, acidic tomatoes, and herbs to complement the bitter flavors of the smoked ribs. This sauce goes with just about any side dish you'd consider serving, from grilled corn, to roasted mushrooms, or crispy potatoes.

BARBACOA RUB
2 tablespoons (12 g) black pepper
1 teaspoon ground cumin
⅓ cup (75 g) kosher salt
¼ cup (28 g) smoked paprika
3 tablespoons (24 g) guajillo chile
   powder
2 tablespoons (6 g) dried Mexican
   oregano
2 teaspoons granulated garlic
1 teaspoon chipotle chile powder
1 teaspoon dried thyme
½ teaspoon ground cinnamon

RIBS
1 section beef plate ribs,
   4–5 pounds (1.8–2.3 kg)
¼ cup (44 g) yellow mustard
   Barbacoa Rub
½ cup (120 ml) apple cider vinegar

BARBACOA SAUCE
5 dried guajillo chiles
1 dried ancho chile
2 plum tomatoes
2 large tomatillos
¼ white onion
2 garlic cloves, in husk
1 teaspoon sesame seeds
¼ teaspoon ground cumin
¼ teaspoon dried thyme
½ cup (120 ml) beef stock
Kosher salt

EQUIPMENT
Spray bottle
Pink butcher paper

INSTRUCTIONS
Preheat the smoker to 275°F (140°C).

In a small bowl, stir together the ingredients together for the *Barbacoa Rub*. Taste and adjust as needed.

Trim any silver skin and excess fat off of the top of the beef ribs. Slather the yellow mustard all over the ribs, which will help the seasoning stick. Apply the *Barbacoa Rub* generously on all sides and let the beef rest at room temperature while the smoker comes to temp.

Place the ribs on the smoker, bone-side down, and allow them to smoke undisturbed for 2 hours. Spritz the outside of the ribs ➤➤

with apple cider vinegar as needed to keep them moist, every 45 minutes after the first few hours. Continue to smoke for 6–8 hours.

It's time to prepare the sauce. Preheat the oven's broiler to high. Wipe the chiles clean and remove the stems and seeds. Place them on a small baking sheet. Broil for about 1 minute. Place the chiles in a large bowl and pour hot water over them, allowing them to hydrate for about 20 minutes.

Arrange the tomatoes, tomatillos, onion, and garlic in an even layer on a large baking sheet. Broil for 6–8 minutes and flip the vegetables. Continue to broil for another 5–6 minutes or until the skins have blistered and are blackened.

Discard the stems and blackened skin from the tomatoes. Remove the garlic and tomatillos from the charred husks. Place everything into the blender with the hydrated chiles, sesame seeds, cumin, thyme, and beef stock. Purée until smooth and adjust with salt as needed.

Check the beef ribs for temperature and feel using a meat thermometer. The probe should slide into the meat with little resistance as if it were creamy peanut butter. The internal temperature should be around 200–205°F (93–96°C), but the feel is more important. Keep it cooking regardless of the temperature if the meat is still tough and shows resistance. Once it's ready, remove the ribs from the smoker and wrap in pink butcher paper to rest for about an hour at room temperature.

Slice through the ribs and serve immediately with a side of the *Barbacoa Sauce*.

VINDALOO-SPICED
LAMB LOLLIPOPS

MAKES
7-8
LAMB
LOLLIPOPS

My first memory of eating lamb was in vindaloo, a very spicy dish I grew to love during my college years. It didn't take long for me to adapt these flavors for over the fire, creating a spicy marinade that can be used for pork, beef, chicken, lamb, or even shrimp. This recipe is incredible with grilled lamb lollipops, but don't stop there. Make sure you whip up the spicy herb sauce, which also pairs well when making *Tandoori Butterflied Chicken Drumsticks* (page 101).

VINDALOO MARINADE
2 teaspoons cumin seeds
2 teaspoons coriander seeds
1 tablespoon (10 g) black peppercorns
4 whole cloves
8–10 dried chile de árbol peppers
   (adjust for heat level)
1 teaspoon paprika
1 teaspoon brown sugar
½ teaspoon ground cinnamon
8 garlic cloves, peeled
2 tablespoons (12 g) chopped fresh
   ginger
¼ cup (60 ml) distilled
   white vinegar
1 cup (235 ml) water

LAMB
1 Frenched lamb rib rack, with
   7–8 ribs each
½ tablespoon kosher salt

COCONUT HERB
YOGURT SAUCE
2 jalapeño peppers, chopped, seeds
   optional
4 scallions, chopped
1 cup (16 g) chopped fresh cilantro
1 cup (96 g) chopped fresh mint
½ cup (120 ml) coconut milk
½ cup (115 g) Greek yogurt
1 teaspoon white sugar
Juice of 1 lemon
½ teaspoon kosher salt, plus more
   as needed

INSTRUCTIONS
Prepare the marinade by preheating a skillet over medium heat. Toast the cumin seeds, coriander seeds, black peppercorns, cloves, and dried chile de árbol peppers for 2–3 minutes until they are aromatic. Make sure to stir the spices and chiles so they do not burn. Transfer the spices and the rest of the ingredients for the marinade to a high-speed blender and purée until smooth.

Slice the lamb ribs between the bones into individual lollipops, which should give you 7–8 of them depending on the rack. Lightly salt each side of the lamb and place it in a resealable container. Pour the cooled marinade into the container, rubbing the lollipops to make sure each is fully coated with the sauce. Allow to marinate in the fridge for at least 4–6 hours.

Prepare the yogurt sauce. Place the jalapeño peppers, scallions, and herbs into a food processor. Blitz until the ingredients form a smooth paste, adding a splash of water if needed. In a small bowl, mix the coconut milk and yogurt together and then stir in the jalapeño paste, sugar, lemon juice, and salt. Adjust with additional salt as needed. Place in the fridge until ready to use.

Preheat the grill for direct cooking at high heat, 450–500°F (230–250°C). Clean the grill grates and oil them ➤➤

as needed. Remove the lamb from the marinade and brush off any excess. Allow the lamb to rest at room temperature while the grill is preheating.

Place the lamb directly over the coals and press down with tongs. Allow the lamb to sear for 5 minutes to build a quick crust without overcooking. Flip and cook for another 4–5 minutes, building up another side of grill marks. Make sure the fat cap on the outside is seared as well, which will create a delicious crispy bite. For medium-rare, remove the lamb when it hits about 130°F (54°C).

Let the meat rest for 5 minutes. Grab a lamb lollipop and serve with the herbaceous *Coconut Herb Yogurt Sauce*.

NOTE: Applewood smoke works very well with this recipe. I highly recommend using some wood chips right before searing the lamb. Sprinkle some directly on the coals and let them ignite before adding the lamb to the grill.

SMOKED LAMB
BARBACOA BANH MI

SERVES
6–8
PEOPLE

Banh mi flavors and textures create one of the most exciting sandwiches, pairing warm meats with sweet, sour, and spicy flavor profiles. Slow-smoked lamb pairs perfectly with pickled vegetables and fresh herbs, sandwiched between two slices of crusty bread. This adobo-rubbed leg of lamb is smoked to a temperature similar to that of roast beef and then sliced thin for sandwiches. Use any bread you can find with a soft interior and a thin, crisp crust.

LAMB BARBACOA
1 boneless leg of lamb, 3–4 pounds
   (1.4–1.8 kg)
2 teaspoons kosher salt
1 cup (240 g) *Arizona Adobo Sauce*
   (page 41)

SPRITZ
½ cup (120 ml) apple cider vinegar

SANDWICH
6–8 baguettes, tortas, or bolillo rolls
1 cup (225 g) *Smoked Garlic Aioli*
   (page 37)
2 cups (448 g) *Hot Pickled Red Onions*
   (page 48)
2 English cucumbers, sliced into coins
4 jalapeño peppers, sliced into rings
1 bunch fresh basil leaves
1 bunch fresh cilantro
Soy sauce for seasoning

EQUIPMENT
Kitchen twine
Spray bottle

INSTRUCTIONS

Trim any excess fat or silver skin from the outside of the lamb. Season the lamb with salt and then rub the *Arizona Adobo Sauce* over the entire surface to coat it. Roll the meat back into the original roast shape and use kitchen twine to tie it into place. Cover the lamb and place it in the refrigerator for at least 4 hours, up to overnight.

Preheat the smoker to 250°F (120°C). This lamb tastes particularly great with apple-wood or hickory wood. Take the lamb out of the fridge and allow it to warm at room temperature while the smoker heats up.

Place the tied lamb leg on the smoker, allowing it to cook undisturbed for an hour. Check on it, spritzing the edges with apple cider vinegar as needed to keep it moist. Continue to smoke until the internal temperature in the thickest part reads 140°F (60°C). Remove it from the smoker and allow it to rest for 10–15 minutes.

Slice the lamb into very thin slices when ready to assemble. Cut open the sandwich rolls and scrape out a little of the bread from the inside, allowing more room for the fillings. Smear the *Smoked Garlic Aioli* on the inside of the rolls, topping with a generous portion of the smoked lamb, *Hot Pickled Red Onions*, cucumbers, jalapeño peppers, basil, and cilantro. Drizzle on a little soy sauce to season.

WINGS, TINGA & OTHER CHICKEN DISHES

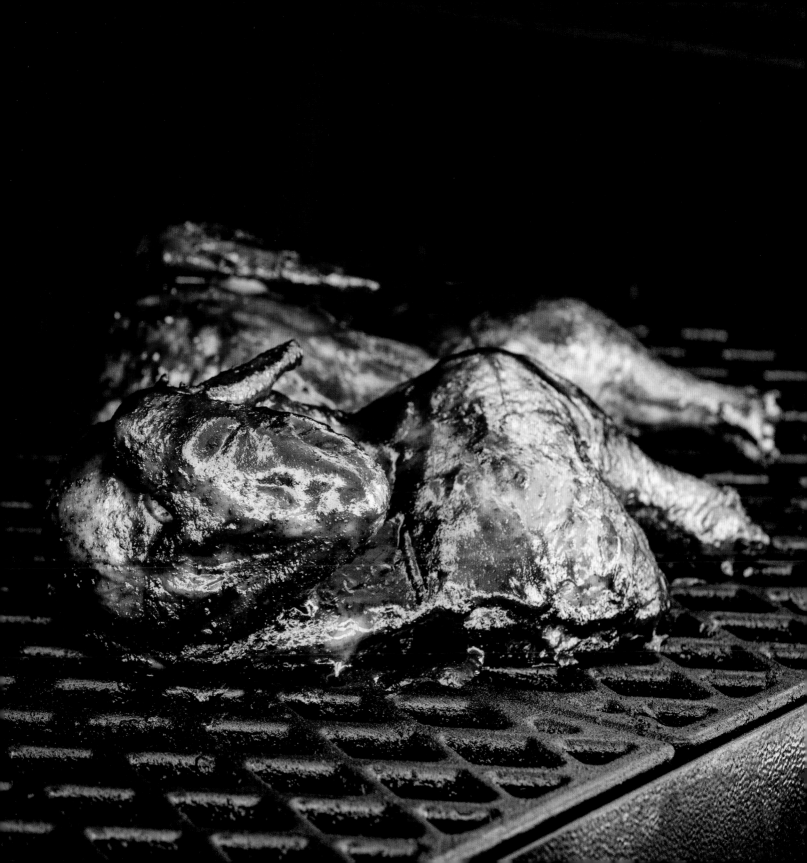

GRILLED CHICKEN FAJITA
WEDGE SALAD

<table>
<tr><td>SERVES
ABOUT
4
PEOPLE</td></tr>
</table>

Eating in the Southwest means you'll run across fajitas pretty often. Steak, chicken, or shrimp are grilled and served with a medley of sautéed peppers and onions. This recipe came about when I found myself eating fajita leftovers with a salad, realizing this would be a delicious intentional combination. This wedge salad skips over the pan, cooking the marinated veggies and chicken directly on the grill. Searing the onions and peppers draws out their natural sweetness and provides charred texture and aromas. Chicken breasts are scored and spiced with a mix of chili powder, ginger, and turmeric, showcasing that flavorful, glowing orange color. Sure, you could grab some tortillas, but grilled romaine lettuce provides the perfect crispy bed for everything to lay on. Drizzle with your dressing of choice, though I'll provide a couple suggestions from elsewhere in the book.

2 boneless, skinless chicken breasts, 4–5 ounces (115–140 g) each

FAJITA MARINADE
1½ tablespoons (12 g) *Light Chili Powder* (page 31)
1 teaspoon kosher salt
½ teaspoon chipotle chile powder
½ teaspoon ground turmeric
½ teaspoon ground ginger
Juice of 2 limes
1 tablespoon (15 ml) olive oil, plus more as needed

GRILLED VEGETABLES
1 red bell pepper
1 red onion
2 tablespoons (28 ml) olive oil
2 tablespoons (28 ml) red wine vinegar
¼ teaspoon fine sea salt

¼ teaspoon fresh ground black pepper
2 jalapeño peppers, halved lengthwise
1 tablespoon (15 ml) olive oil
2 heads Romaine lettuce, quartered lengthwise

FOR SERVING
Lime Crema (page 110; optional)
Mojo Rojo Sauce (page 167; optional)
Cotija cheese, crumbled

INSTRUCTIONS
Using a sharp knife, make parallel, shallow cuts approximately ⅛ inch (3 mm) deep and ½ inch (1.3 cm) apart, creating a crosshatch on both sides of the chicken breasts. Mix the marinade ingredients together in a small bowl. Place the chicken breasts in a plastic bag and pour in the

marinade, mixing to coat the chicken. Allow the chicken to marinate in the fridge for at least an hour, up to overnight.

Slice the red bell pepper and red onion into rings about ¼ inch (6 mm) thick. Mix the olive oil, red wine vinegar, salt, and pepper in a small bowl. Place the bell pepper and red onion in a sealed container or bag, pour in the mixture, and allow to marinate in the fridge for at least an hour, up to overnight.

Prepare the grill for a 2-zone cooking setup at medium-high heat, 350–400°F (180–200°C), with the hot coals on one side. Clean the grill grates and oil them as needed. Take the chicken out of the fridge while the grill warms up. ➤➤

Wipe off any excess marinade and place the chicken on the grill directly over the coals and allow it to grill for 4–5 minutes on each side. Cook for an additional 5–6 minutes. If the chicken is getting crispy but not fully cooked through, move to the cooler side of the grill and close the lid for a few minutes until it comes up to a temperature of 160°F (71°C). Remove the chicken from the grill and allow it to rest with loosely tented foil for about 15 minutes, bringing it up to 165°F (74°C).

Grill the jalapeño peppers and marinated onion and bell pepper slices directly over the heat. Flip every couple of minutes as you start to see some char. Remove the vegetables and set aside when they are cooked to your preference.

Lightly oil the cut side of the romaine lettuce and set directly on the grill for about 2 minutes per side, flipping as needed. The romaine will slightly char and wilt.

Dress your plates with romaine lettuce, sliced chicken, grilled onions and peppers, and dressing of choice. I recommend garnishing with a crumbly, salty cheese such as Cotija.

NASHVILLE HOT
BBQ CHICKEN

Everyone traveling to Nashville needs to stop and order plenty of hot chicken. When I stopped by, Derek Wolf, from Over the Fire Cooking, took me around the town to try as many places as we could. He also shared his personal recipe, which he is pretty well known for. The variety around town when it came to the hot chicken really surprised me. There were big differences between all of the dry rubs, sauces, and brines. I knew I had to transport these flavors to my grill. This recipe uses a split whole chicken, brined with pickle juice before slowly smoking it with a blend of hot chiles. One layer of heat isn't enough, so the chicken is glazed with a rich, spicy Nashville hot barbecue sauce toward the end. Grab an ice-cold beer. You're going to need it for this one.

1 whole chicken, 4–5 pounds (1.8–2.3 kg)
2 cups (475 ml) brine from jarred dill pickles
1 tablespoon (15 ml) canola oil

NASHVILLE HOT RUB
½ cup (70 g) *Brad's Smoke Rub* (page 34)
1 tablespoon (5 g) cayenne pepper

NASHVILLE HOT BBQ SAUCE
1½ cups (360 g) ketchup
3 tablespoons (45 ml) apple cider vinegar
2 tablespoons (28 ml) Worcestershire sauce
¼ cup (60 g) brown sugar
½ tablespoon cayenne pepper
1 teaspoon guajillo chile powder
1 teaspoon smoked paprika
1 teaspoon chipotle chile powder

1 teaspoon garlic powder
2 teaspoons yellow mustard
1 teaspoon kosher salt
3 tablespoons (60 g) molasses

FOR SERVING
Sliced white bread
Nashville Hot BBQ Sauce
Dill pickles,
Pickled Jalapeños (page 46)
Hot Pickled Red Onions (page 48)

INSTRUCTIONS
Split the chicken in half. Cut along each side of the backbone with shears to remove it. Use a chef's knife to make a score on the center of the breastbone on the inside. Flip the chicken over so the skin side is facing up. Using the heel of your hand, press down firmly on the center of the breast and you'll hear a snap.

Make sure the chicken skin is evenly distributed across the front of the breasts. Place your knife in the middle of the breasts to divide the chicken in half and firmly press down through the meat, cutting through some bone. Now, there are two halves, and you're ready to brine.

Place the halves in a large resealable bag and add the pickle brine. Seal the bag, leaving just the last inch (2.5 cm) open. Slowly lower the bag into a pot of water. As you lower the bag, the pressure will push the oxygen out. Just before you fully submerge the bag, seal off the opening and pull the bag out of the water. Place the brined chicken in the fridge to marinate for at least 3 hours, up to overnight. ➼

Remove the chicken from the brine and pat dry. Brush the oil lightly over the chicken. This will help the skin crisp up nicely and allow the seasoning to adhere. Prepare the rub by mixing *Brad's Smoke Rub* with the cayenne pepper in a small bowl. Sprinkle the *Nashville Hot Rub* generously on all sides and allow the chicken to rest while the smoker warms up.

Prepare the smoker for indirect cooking at 300°F (150°C). Use a mild wood, such as oak or fruitwood.

Place the chicken skin-side up on the grates and close the smoker. Allow the chicken to smoke undisturbed for about an hour while you prepare the sauce.

Whisk together all of the ingredients for the barbecue sauce in a medium-size saucepan over medium heat. Once the ingredients boil, reduce the heat to low and simmer for 6–8 minutes. Stir occasionally and add a teaspoon of water if it becomes too thick. Taste and adjust. Remove from the heat when ready.

Check on the chicken. When the breast meat reaches an internal temperature of 150°F (66°C), glaze all sides of the chicken with the sauce and continue to cook. Remove the chicken from the smoker when the breast meat reaches 160°F (71°C). Loosely tent the chicken with aluminum foil and allow it to rest for about 15 minutes, bringing it up to 165°F (74°C).

Slice when ready and serve with white bread, extra *Nashville Hot BBQ Sauce*, and pickled vegetables.

CHIPOTLE TAHINI
GRILLED CHICKEN

SERVES
4–6
PEOPLE

The simple sauce in this recipe is something I've used over the years to create big flavors without having to overcomplicate a meal. Tahini and soy sauce are the foundation, creating a savory profile that is fortified with smoky chipotles, orange juice, and aromatics. The smell of charred tahini and chicken skin dripping down into the coals is intoxicating, so thankfully, these don't take too long to cook. Serve with a side of marinated onions to brighten the palate as you eat. While this recipe uses chicken legs, I've found it also works well with wings or even bone-in chicken breasts. I highly recommend pairing this chicken with the *Harissa Sweet Potato Salad* (page 163) or *Southwest Creamed Corn* (page 173) for a complete meal.

CHIPOTLE TAHINI CHICKEN

4 pounds (1.8 kg) bone-in chicken legs

1 cup (235 ml) canola oil

½ cup (120 ml) orange juice

½ cup (120 g) tahini

5 chipotle chiles in adobo sauce

¼ cup (60 ml) soy sauce

5 garlic cloves

2 tablespoons (16 g) toasted sesame seeds

Slices of lemon (optional)

¼ cup (16 g) fresh flat-leaf parsley, chopped

MARINATED ONIONS

2 tablespoons (28 ml) olive oil

2 tablespoons (28 ml) fresh lemon juice

2 tablespoons (28 ml) red wine vinegar

1 tablespoon (8) ground sumac

½ teaspoon white sugar

½ teaspoon kosher salt, plus more as needed

1 red onion, thinly sliced

2 tablespoons (8 g) fresh flat leaf parsley, chopped

INSTRUCTIONS

Pat the chicken dry. Using a sharp paring knife, cut parallel slashes into the chicken about 1 inch (2.5 cm) apart, all the way to the bone on both sides of the legs.

Combine the canola oil, orange juice, tahini, chipotle chiles, soy sauce, and garlic in a high-speed blender and purée until smooth. Place the chicken in a sealed plastic bag or container. Pour in the marinade and rub the chicken to make sure it's evenly coated. Allow the chicken to marinate in the fridge for at least 2 hours, up to 6.

Prepare the onions. In a small bowl, whisk together the olive oil, lemon juice, red wine vinegar, sumac, sugar, and salt. Taste and adjust with more salt if needed. In a medium-size bowl, combine the red onion, dressing, and parsley, tossing to combine. Allow these to marinate in the fridge for at least an hour.

Remove the chicken from the marinade and wipe off excess sauce.

Prepare the grill for a 2-zone cooking setup at medium-high heat, 350–400°F (180–200°C), with the hot coals on one side. I recommend adding hardwood to the charcoal, such as apple or hickory.

Clean and oil the grill grates when ready. Place the chicken skin-side down directly

over the coals and grill for 5–6 minutes until the chicken is seared and releases from the grates. Flip and cook for another 5–6 minutes to sear the other side. Move the chicken to the cooler side of the grill when ready and close the lid, allowing the chicken to finish cooking for another 10 minutes or until the meat registers at least 170°F (77°C).

Remove the chicken from the grill and allow it to rest for 5–10 minutes. Serve with the *Marinated Onions* and garnish with sesame seeds. Squeeze a slice of lemon over the chicken and garnish with parsley before serving.

TANDOORI BUTTERFLIED
CHICKEN DRUMSTICKS

SERVES
4–5
PEOPLE

Tandoori chicken searing over hot coals has to be one of my favorite grilling smells. Bold spices and chiles char alongside the juicy chicken dripping into the coals, creating incredible aromas. This marinated chicken is grilled hot and fast, creating a crust on the outside while keeping the meat juicy. I've been working on my personal tandoori masala recipe for years. It's actually one of the first Indian-inspired dishes that landed on my grill. I found that Kashmiri chiles have a mild heat with fruity flavors, similar to guajillo chiles, which are fresh and abundant where I live (so I usually go with them). Achiote paste is sweet and bright red, helping stain the chicken without the use of food coloring. Butterflied chicken drumsticks work very well for this process, cooking faster with much more flavor than white meat. Plus, food always tastes better on a stick, right?

10 chicken drumsticks, about
   2½ pounds (1.1 kg)

FIRST MARINADE
2 teaspoons guajillo chile powder
1 tablespoon (8 g) grated fresh ginger
1 tablespoon (10 g) grated garlic
1 tablespoon (15 ml) fresh lemon juice
1 teaspoon salt

SECOND MARINADE
1¼ cups (290 g) Greek yogurt
1 tablespoon (8 g) guajillo chile
   powder
1 tablespoon (16 g) achiote paste
1 tablespoon (8 g) grated fresh ginger
1 tablespoon (10 g) grated garlic
2 teaspoons paprika
1 teaspoon ground cumin
1 teaspoon ground coriander
1 teaspoon salt

FOR SERVING
½ red onion, thinly sliced
Chopped fresh cilantro
Coconut Herb Yogurt Sauce (page 85)

INSTRUCTIONS
Pat the chicken drumsticks dry. Place a drumstick on your cutting board, with the side that has the most meat showing facing up. Using a sharp knife, cut the meat along one side of the bone, careful not to slice all the way through. Make a second cut, separating the meat from the other side of the bone. Fold open the meat and lay the drumstick facedown. Carefully remove the chicken skin from the back of the drumstick and discard. Repeat for each one.

In a large bowl, mix together the ingredients for the first marinade. Add the chicken and mix it very well, making sure to completely coat all of the meat. This will be easy to tell, as it's bright red. Cover the bowl with plastic wrap and let it marinate for 45–60 minutes in the fridge.

In a second large bowl, mix the ingredients for the second marinade. After the first marination time has passed, transfer the chicken directly into the second bowl. Mix again to coat the chicken completely and allow it to marinate in the fridge for at least 6 hours, up to overnight.

When ready to grill, take the bowl of chicken out of the fridge about 30 minutes before cooking. Preheat the grill ➥

for direct cooking at high heat, 450–500°F (230–250°C). Make sure to clean the grill grates well, rubbing them with a little oil to help prevent the meat from sticking. This step is very important, as the yogurt marinade will otherwise caramelize onto the grill grates.

Shake off excess marinade from the chicken and place it directly over the coals. Close the lid and allow the chicken to cook for 5–6 minutes. Carefully check the drumsticks to see if they are ready to flip. They should release fairly easily from the grill. Cook for an additional 5–6 minutes on the second side and continue to flip as needed to finish them. The finished temperature should be at least 170°F (77°C), which is where the meat will be crispier and start to fall off the bone.

Serve with sliced red onion, cilantro, and a side of the *Coconut Herb Yogurt Sauce.*

GRILLED ADOBO-RUBBED CHICKEN
WITH CREAMY HERB SAUCE

Walking by the markets in Phoenix, you'll almost always see a smoldering open charcoal grill lined up with brightly-colored chickens. Orange and red marinades glow, giving off an incredible aroma of charred chicken skin and chiles. It's impossible to walk by without wishing you could stop and eat. Fortunately, you have this book, and this adobo-rubbed chicken is going to satisfy that dream. Prepare the *Arizona Adobo Sauce* and you're ready to go. The *Creamy Herb Sauce* adds a rich, fatty, and vibrant flavor to counter that bitter char from the chiles. I recommend serving this with a side of the *Crispy Skillet Potatoes* (page 167) to dip in the sauce as well.

1 whole chicken, 3½–4 pounds
   (1.6–1.8 g)
1 cup (240 g) *Arizona Adobo Sauce*
   (page 41)
1 teaspoon kosher salt
1 tablespoon (15 ml) canola oil

CREAMY HERB SAUCE
12 fresh basil leaves
½ cup (8 g) chopped fresh cilantro
4 scallions, roughly chopped
1 avocado, cubed
¾ cup (175 g) *Smoked Garlic Aioli*
   (page 37)
Juice of 1 lime
Kosher salt

INSTRUCTIONS

Cut the backbone out of the chicken using a sharp pair of poultry shears or kitchen scissors. Start at the tail end and work upward, snipping through the rib bones as you go. Remove the backbone and flip the chicken over so the inside is facing down. Spread the chicken out carefully and push firmly in the middle of the breast—you should hear a snap. Now the chicken is spatchcocked and ready to go.

In a small bowl, mix the *Arizona Adobo Sauce* with the salt and oil. Using gloves or a pastry brush, baste the entire chicken with the adobo sauce. You can prep the chicken a few hours ahead of time if you'd prefer, keeping it covered in the fridge. Just take it out of the fridge about 30 minutes before you start the grill.

Prepare the grill for a 2-zone cooking setup at medium-high heat, 350–400°F (180–200°C), with the hot coals on one side. The chicken will be grilled directly and then finished on the other side. ➤➤

Prepare the herb sauce while the grill preheats. Place all ingredients in a blender and purée until completely smooth, thinning with a bit of water if it's too thick. Taste and adjust with salt as needed. Place in the fridge until ready to use.

Clean the grill grates and oil them as needed. Place the chicken skin-side down directly over the coals, pressing to make sure it's completely flat. Grill the chicken with the lid open for 5–7 minutes, until there are visible grill marks and the skin starts to crisp. Flip the chicken carefully with tongs and cook for another 5–7 minutes on the other side.

Transfer the chicken to the cooler side of the grill, with the breasts facing the coals. Close the lid of the grill and continue to cook for 20 minutes. Check on the chicken and rotate it, so the breasts are facing away from the coals, and continue to cook for another 20–30 minutes until the internal temperature in the breast reads about 160°F (71°C). Remove the chicken from the grill and allow it to rest with loosely tented foil for about 15 minutes, bringing it up to 165°F (74°C).

Transfer the chicken to a cutting board and allow it to rest for about 10 minutes before carving. Serve with the *Creamy Herb Sauce*.

ADAPTABLE ADOBO

Many traditional Mexican dishes start with an adobo sauce. This magic chile paste can be used to marinate or braise many different cuts of meats. Allow your pork chops, chicken wings, or shrimp to marinate for a couple of hours and then toss them on the grill. Mix a few cups (720–960 g) with ground pork or beef, and you'll have homemade chorizo. Braise short ribs with beef broth and adobo sauce for a few hours, and you'll have a rich *birria* for tacos.

Many authentic varieties exist, but the *Arizona Adobo Sauce* was designed with barbecue and grilling in mind. When grilling, heat from the coals chars and caramelizes this sauce on the outside, creating a delicious, browned crust. Simply add some salt to your meat and slather it with a generous layer of the adobo sauce.

The same principle works for low and slow barbecue. Seasoning the meat with salt and adobo sauce creates a dark, rich bark on the outside. The fragrant smoke is absorbed into the surface, deepening the already toasty flavors.

Try out different plating combinations, but make sure that you pair the meat with something bright and vibrant to counter the savory roasted chiles.

GRILLED
CHICKEN TINGA

SERVES

6-8

PEOPLE

This spicy, savory shredded chicken, slowly braised in a thick sauce, just might be your new week-night go-to. Searing the chicken first adds a delicious wood-fired layer of flavor to the sauce while braising. The homemade adobo sauce is the power move, adding a spicy depth to the dish. Typically, I'll turn these into tacos, topping them with *Hot Pickled Red Onions* (page 48) and plenty of lime. But I've also been known to make pulled chicken sandwiches, which are amazing when topped with plenty of *Pickled Sweet Bell Peppers* (page 45).

INGREDIENTS

8 bone-in, skin-on chicken thighs,
    about 4½ ounces (125 g) each
3 tablespoons (45 ml) vegetable oil
1 tablespoon (14 g) kosher salt,
    plus more as needed
1 tablespoon (7 g) paprika
1 tablespoon (6 g) black pepper
4 Roma tomatoes
2 tomatillos
½ medium white onion, finely diced
2 jalapeño peppers, seeded and finely
    diced
½ cup (120 g) *Arizona Adobo Sauce*
    (page 41)
¾ cup (175 ml) chicken stock

INSTRUCTIONS

Brush the chicken thighs with 2 tablespoons (28 ml) of oil and season liberally with the salt, paprika, and pepper on all sides.

Preheat the grill for direct cooking at medium heat, 300–350°F (150–180°C). Clean the grill grates and oil them as needed.

Sear the chicken thighs on the grill, skin-side down for 4–5 minutes until a nice char develops. Flip the chicken and repeat on the other side for another 5 minutes. Remove the chicken and set aside.

Grill the whole tomatoes and tomatillos for a few minutes until just bursting. Remove and set aside to cool. Remove the skins of the tomatoes and dice them up along with the tomatillos.

Heat up a 4-quart (3.8 L) Dutch oven directly over the coals. Add the remaining tablespoon (15 ml) of oil to the pot, giving it time to heat up and shimmer. Cook the onion and jalapeño peppers in the hot oil for 2 minutes until they are softened. Add the tomatoes and tomatillos and allow them to cook down for 2 minutes and then add the *Arizona Adobo Sauce*. Continue cooking while stirring for about 5 minutes to incorporate all of the flavors together.

Transfer the sauce to a blender. Carefully purée until smooth and pour the sauce back into the Dutch oven on the grill. Add the chicken stock and stir to combine. Nestle the chicken thighs in the sauce and place the lid on the Dutch oven. Allow everything to cook for 20–30 minutes until the chicken can be easily shredded.

Remove the chicken from the sauce and discard the skin, bones, or any large pieces of fat. Stir the shredded chicken back into the sauce and cook until it's warmed through, about 2 minutes. Remove from the heat and season with salt to taste.

GOCHUJANG HONEY MUSTARD
CHICKEN SANDWICH

MAKES
4
SANDWICHES

I'm a sucker for spicy honey mustard, and my constant tinkering with the condiment eventually led me to this combination of gochujang, mustard, and honey. The savory combination of Dijon and gochujang meld perfectly, with the honey adding just enough sweetness to temper the chiles. This sauce is regularly used for all types of grilled chicken (and shrimp) on our home menu. Scoring the chicken breasts ensures they cook quickly and evenly, also adding more texture and room for plenty of savory sauce. Pair this sandwich with generous portions of the *Creamy Dijon Herb Slaw,* which adds some fat and acidity for an incredibly well-rounded lunch.

GOCHUJANG HONEY MUSTARD

½ cup (120 g) gochujang
¼ cup (60 g) Dijon mustard
1½ tablespoons (25 ml) soy sauce
1½ tablespoons (30 g) honey
2 teaspoons sesame oil

CHICKEN SANDWICH

4 chicken breasts, 4–5 ounces
    (115–140 g) each
1 teaspoon kosher salt
4 potato buns
2 tablespoons (28 g) *Smoked Garlic
    Aioli* (page 37)
Pickled Sweet Bell Peppers (page 45)
2 cups (240 g) *Creamy Dijon Herb
    Slaw* (page 176)

INSTRUCTIONS

Prepare the sauce. In a medium-size bowl, whisk all the honey mustard ingredients together. Add a teaspoon of water at a time to thin out the sauce as needed. It should be slightly thinner than your typical barbecue sauce. Taste and adjust. Set aside half of the sauce.

Prepare the grill for a 2-zone cooking setup at medium-high heat, 350–400°F (180–200°C), with the hot coals on one side. Clean the grill grates and oil them as needed.

Using a sharp knife, make parallel, shallow cuts approximately ⅛ inch (3 mm) deep and ½ inch (1.3 cm) apart, creating a crosshatch on both sides of the chicken breasts. Lightly season both sides with salt. Brush half of the *Gochujang Honey Mustard* on both sides of the chicken and get ready to grill.

Place the chicken breasts on the grill directly over the coals and allow them to grill for 4–5 minutes per side. Cook for an additional 5–6 minutes. If the chicken is getting crispy but not fully cooked through, move to the cooler side of the grill and close the lid for a few minutes until it comes up to a temperature of 160°F (71°C). Remove the chicken from the grill and allow it to rest with loosely tented foil for about 15 minutes, bringing it up to 165°F (74°C).

Toast the buns on the grill briefly and prepare your sandwich. Spread some *Smoked Garlic Aioli* on the bottom bun, top with *Pickled Sweet Bell Peppers,* the chicken breast, and pile on the *Creamy Dijon Herb Slaw.* Pair with an ice-cold beer—this is a spicy one!

ENCHILADA
WINGS

SERVES
ABOUT
2
PEOPLE

If I had to pick a recipe to represent *Chiles and Smoke*, it would probably be these chicken wings. The rich, fruity flavors of the chiles pair with the tangy spicy of the *Guajillo Ketchup* and sweetness of the brown sugar to create a complex barbecue sauce. I remember the first time tasting this, the only thing I could focus on was my desire to buy chicken wings and fire up the grill. Smoked slowly and seared, the wings are basted with the dark sauce and caramelized right over the coals. The smells of roasting chiles will remind you that these are spicy wings, so whip up some *Lime Crema* to cool off.

ENCHILADA BBQ SAUCE
5 dried guajillo chiles, stemmed and seeded
2 dried ancho chiles, stemmed and seeded
6 chile de árbol peppers, stemmed and seeded
4 garlic cloves, diced
1 teaspoon dried Mexican oregano
½ teaspoon dried thyme
½ teaspoon kosher salt, plus more as needed
¼ cup (60 g) brown sugar
½ cup (120 g) *Guajillo Ketchup* (page 39)
1 tablespoon (15 ml) apple cider vinegar
¼ cup (60 ml) water

CHICKEN WINGS
1 tablespoon (7 g) smoked paprika
1 teaspoon garlic powder
2 teaspoons kosher salt
1 teaspoon black pepper

2 pounds (900 g) chicken wings, separated to drums and flats

LIME CREMA
8 ounces (225 g) sour cream
Zest of 1 lime
Juice of 1 lime
¼ teaspoon fine sea salt

FOR GARNISH
Lime wedges
4 tablespoons (32 g) Cotija cheese

INSTRUCTIONS
Prepare the BBQ sauce first. Clean the chiles with a damp paper towel. Heat a cast iron skillet over medium-high heat and toast the chiles, flipping occasionally, until puffed and lightly browned for 4–5 minutes. Place them in a large bowl and pour hot water over them, allowing them to hydrate for about 20 minutes. Drain the chiles and add them to the blender with the rest of the sauce ingredients. Purée until smooth and then pour the sauce into a small saucepan over low heat. Stir and simmer for a few minutes to allow the ingredients to meld into a smooth, velvety sauce. Taste and adjust with salt if needed.

To make the wings, in a large bowl, mix the paprika, garlic powder, salt, and pepper. Season the wings generously and allow them to sit out while you preheat the grill.

Prepare the grill for a 2-zone cooking setup at medium-high heat, 350–400°F (180–200°C), with the hot coals on one side. Optionally, add some hardwood for smoke flavor. I recommend applewood. Clean the grill grates and oil them as needed. ➤➤

Prepare the crema. Mix the crema ingredients together in a small bowl and place in the fridge until ready to use.

Place the wings on the cool side of the grill, allowing them to cook for about 30 minutes before flipping. Keep the lid closed while they are cooking indirectly. Make sure the wings closer to the coals are not cooking faster, rotating them from front to back as needed. You will cook them for 45–60 minutes depending on their size, until they reach 165°F (74°C) internal temperature.

The chicken is ready to be basted with the *Enchilada BBQ Sauce* when they hit 160–165°F (71–74°C). Baste the wings and grill directly over the hot coals. Cook for a couple minutes on each side until you are satisfied with the char. We're looking to grill the wings to a temperature of about 180°F (82°C) internal, which makes them crispier and easier to eat off the bone.

Serve with the cool *Lime Crema* and lime wedges and top with Cotija cheese.

BACON-WRAPPED
CHEESY CHICKEN POBLANOS

SERVES
6-8
PEOPLE

Just about anything filled with cheese and wrapped in bacon could pass for a tasty snack, but these chiles are so much more. Using the larger poblano chiles provides much more space for the fillings and they have a sharp, bitter flavor to contrast with the cheeses. Soft cream cheese is mixed with shredded Gouda for a rich base, and marinated chicken tenders are placed on top. Bacon holds everything together, creating a crispy exterior with every bite while keeping the chicken moist. At my house, we usually serve these as appetizers for a group, but they are filling enough for a meal.

INGREDIENTS

6 chicken tenders, 6–8 ounces
    (170–225 g) each
½ cup (120 ml) pineapple juice
Juice of 2 limes
1 jalapeño pepper, seeded and diced
1 teaspoon kosher salt
½ teaspoon dried Mexican oregano
½ teaspoon ground cumin
6 strips bacon, regular thickness
6 poblano chiles
8 ounces (225 g) cream cheese
1 cup (115 g) shredded cheddar cheese
1 cup (115 g) shredded Monterey Jack
    cheese
2 garlic cloves, minced

INSTRUCTIONS

Place the chicken tenders in a resealable plastic bag. Add the pineapple juice, lime juice, jalapeño pepper, salt, oregano, and cumin. Mix to distribute the spices and coat the chicken. Seal the bag, removing as much air as possible, and place in the fridge to marinate for an hour, up to 4.

Prepare the smoker or grill for indirect cooking at 425°F (220°C). If using a grill, prepare a 2-zone cooking setup, with the hot coals on one side. Clean the grill gates and oil them as needed.

Remove the bacon from the fridge and allow it to come to room temperature. This will allow the bacon to stretch around the poblano chiles more easily.

Set your poblano chiles on a cutting board. Using a small knife, slice across the top about 2 inches (5 cm) and then slice down the length of the chile to remove a wedge about the length of the chicken tender. Remove the seeds and any membrane in the way. This will allow the peppers to hold the cheese and chicken without falling apart. In a medium-size bowl, mix the cheeses and garlic together. Fill each poblano with an even amount of the cheese mixture, pushing it down into the cavities—you'll need enough room to top the cheese with a piece of chicken. ➥

Remove the chicken from the marinade when ready and pat each piece dry. Place a piece of chicken on top of the cheese, pushing it down into the cavity of the pepper. Starting at the chicken, wrap a piece of bacon all the way around the poblanos, stretching slightly to have as many wraps as possible. You may use a toothpick to secure it if needed.

Place the wrapped peppers carefully onto the grill grates. Allow them to roast undisturbed for 35–40 minutes before you check on them. Check the temperature on the chicken, which should be at least 160°F (71°C) degrees. Continue cooking for another 10–15 minutes to crisp up the bacon as needed.

Remove and allow to cool for a few minutes before serving.

NOTE: This recipe is pretty rich, and I've found through testing that less is more when it comes to the bacon. We tend to see jalapeño poppers completely encased in bacon, looking like smoked armadillos. Tasty, but for this recipe, the bacon fat tends to render down and pool inside with the chicken and cheese. Use more at your discretion.

GRILLED STUFFED PEPPERS

Stuffed chiles are very common in the world of barbecue. Simple to prepare, they are a great way to feed a small crowd. The essence of the chiles intensifies when exposed to heat, bringing out more of the sweet, spicy, and bitter flavor profiles. Thick-walled poblanos and bell peppers are some of the most commonly used chiles due to their durability and juiciness.

These larger poblanos make a heavy appetizer but can easily be switched out for different varieties. Try using the same combination of cheeses with *Smoky Southwest Harissa* (page 42), chicken, and parsley packed into red bell peppers for a Mediterranean twist. Shredded *Nashville Hot BBQ Chicken* (page 95) mixed with cream cheese and scallions and stuffed inside jalapeños is a spice *explosion* and one of my personal favorites.

SPICY ORANGE
CHICKEN WINGS

SERVES
1-2
PEOPLE

Sweet and sour flavors of orange chicken remind me of childhood trips to the mall with my mom, when we'd share a giant pile of it for lunch. The combination of flavors has always reminded me a bit of barbecue sauce: sweet heat with savory hints from the smoked or grilled meats. I've made many versions of orange chicken sauces over the years, but the combination of crisp orange soda and savory gochujang creates a vibrant, mouthwatering, sweet hot sauce that you just can't put down. (And you shouldn't!) Fire up your grill and pop open that soda can. It's time.

1 tablespoon (7 g) paprika
1 teaspoon garlic powder
2 teaspoons kosher salt
1 teaspoon black pepper
2 pounds (900 g) chicken wings,
    separated to drums and flats

SPICY ORANGE SAUCE
1 cup (235 ml) orange soda
2 tablespoons (40 g) honey
2 tablespoons (28 g) unsalted butter
2 tablespoons (28 ml) soy sauce
1 tablespoon (15 g) gochujang
1 garlic clove, grated
½ teaspoon grated fresh ginger
1 teaspoon rice wine vinegar
1 tablespoon (8 g) cornstarch

FOR GARNISH
1 scallion, thinly sliced
1 tablespoon (8 g) sesame seeds

INSTRUCTIONS

In a large bowl, mix the paprika, garlic powder, salt, and pepper for the wings. Season the wings generously and allow them to sit at room temperature while you preheat the grill.

Prepare the grill for a 2-zone cooking setup at medium-high heat, 350–400°F (180–200°C), with the hot coals on one side. Optionally, add some hardwood for smoke flavor. Clean the grill grates and oil them as needed.

Place the wings on the cool side of the grill, allowing them to cook for about 30 minutes before flipping. Keep the lid closed while they are cooking indirectly. Make sure the wings closer to the coals are not cooking faster, rotating them from front to back as needed. You will cook them for 45–60 minutes depending on their size, until they reach 165°F (74°C) internal temperature.

Prepare the sauce while the wings are cooking. Add the sauce ingredients to a small saucepan and whisk to incorporate. Place the pan on the grill over the coals, stirring as it cooks and thickens. The sauce will come together after 5–6 minutes.

Check the temperature of the wings, waiting for them to reach 165°F (74°C). Set the sauce aside and grill the wings directly over the coals for 2–3 minutes, flipping as needed. We're looking to grill the wings to a temperature of about 180°F (82°C) internally, which makes them crispier and easier to eat off the bone. Remove the wings and toss them in a bowl with the sauce. Garnish with sliced scallions and sesame seeds.

NOTE: Use your favorite orange soda, but make sure it's room temperature when you're preparing the sauce. My personal choice is Fanta, which has a strong, sweet orange flavor, almost like a mandarin orange. The sauce will thicken as it cools, so don't let it get away from you on the grill. Add a little water if it becomes too thick

WINGS, TINGA & OTHER CHICKEN DISHES

RIBS, CHORIZO & EVERYTHING PORK

CRISPY PORK BELLY
WITH RED CHIMICHURRI

SERVES
ABOUT

6

PEOPLE

The first time I made grilled pork belly, it was due to a happy mistake in my backyard. Caught up in documenting a smoked pork belly with my camera, there was a huge flare up. When removing my grill lid, the fat dripping down hit the charcoal and all of a sudden, it was time to grill. With some quick work from the tongs, the charred pork was flipped and saved. The result was that the tender pork on the inside was sealed with a smoky, crispy bark on the outside, which I couldn't help but make again . . . with intention. This recipe has come a long way, and now I pair it with *Red Chimichurri*, immediately applied after slicing to allow the pork to soak up the vibrant flavors. The acidic sauce cuts through the rich bites, seasoning the meat while allowing the natural pork flavors to shine. This is one of those meals you should eat with friends directly from a cutting board with some ice-cold beers.

RED CHIMICHURRI
1 red bell pepper
½ cup (8 g) chopped fresh cilantro
1 cup (60 g) chopped fresh flat-leaf
    parsley
1 tablespoon (15 g) finely diced
    chipotle chiles in adobo
1 tablespoon (3 g) dried Mexican
    oregano
1 tablespoon (7 g) smoked paprika
½ teaspoon red pepper flakes
2 tablespoons (20 g) minced shallot
4 garlic cloves, minced
2 tablespoons (28 ml) red wine
    vinegar
½ cup (120 g) extra-virgin olive oil
½ teaspoon kosher salt, plus more
    as needed
½ teaspoon black pepper

PORK BELLY
1 pork belly slab, 4–5 pounds
    (1.8–2.3 kg), skin removed
¾ cup (104 g) *Brad's Smoke Rub*
    (page 34)

INSTRUCTIONS
Prepare the chimichurri, which can be made ahead of time. Preheat the grill for direct cooking at a medium heat, 300–350°F (150–180°C). Clean the grill grates and oil them as needed. Place the red bell pepper directly over the flames. Char the bell pepper until the skin is dark and blistered. Remove from the grill and place in a plastic bag or sealed container to steam and soften. Once cooled, discard the charred skin, stems, and seeds. Finely dice and place in a large bowl.

Mix the rest of the chimichurri ingredients into the bowl except for the olive oil, salt, and pepper. Stir to combine and then whisk in the oil and season with salt and pepper as needed. Taste and adjust. Place in the fridge until ready to use.

Prepare the pork belly. Trim the pork of any excess meat or fat from the sides and remove the skin if necessary. Place the pork fat-side up on the cutting board. Using a sharp knife, make vertical slices in the pork belly 1 inch (2.5 cm) apart, slicing almost halfway through the meat. Season the meat generously with *Brad's Smoke Rub* on all sides, making sure the seasoning also gets into the cracks.

Place the pork belly on a wire rack uncovered in the fridge for at least 4 hours, up to overnight. This step will give you a much better bark during the smoking phase.

When ready to cook, remove the pork belly from the fridge and gently pat dry any moisture on the outside.

Prepare the smoker for indirect cooking at 275°F (140°C).

Place the pork belly fat-side up in the smoker and cook for 2–3 hours or until it reaches 195°F (91°C) internal temperature.

Remove the pork belly and allow it to rest while you increase the temperature of the grill for searing. Aim high for 450–500°F (230–250°C). Grill the pork belly meat-side down for about 2 minutes before flipping. Sear the fat side for about 2 minutes or so, being careful of flare ups.

Rest the pork belly for about 10 minutes before cutting on the vertical into slices. Immediately glaze the slices with the *Red Chimichurri*, allowing the flavors to absorb while the pork is hot.

NOTE: This pork is prepared using a method called "dry-brining." Seasoning the meat ahead of time and allowing it to rest in the fridge creates a few benefits when smoking or grilling. The salt draws out excess moisture from the meat, dissolves, and is drawn back into the meat. This also creates a dry surface on the outside, which is ideal for creating a crispier bark. Try this with any larger cut of meat such as a brisket, pork shoulder, or even a porterhouse steak.

SMOKED PORK STEAKS
WITH HARISSA HABANERO BUTTER

SERVES
6–8
PEOPLE

Step aside pork belly, these steaks are hands down my favorite pork-based bite in the world of barbecue. I'm hoping this recipe will help bring pork steaks into the spotlight; they deserve it. Crispy, smoky, and incredibly tender, these basted steaks are finished with an explosion of spices from the *Harissa Habanero Butter*. This is a rich meal, so make sure you have plenty of pickles or salsa handy. Be sure to wear gloves when handling the habanero peppers.

4 pork steaks, 1½-inch (3.8 cm) thick, about 20 ounces (560 g)
Yellow mustard, for coating
¾ cup (104 g) *Brad's Smoke Rub* (page 34)

BASTING SAUCE
4 cups (946 ml) water
1 cup (160 g) chopped shallots, about 2 shallots
2 tablespoons (28 g) unsalted butter
¼ cup (60 ml) apple cider vinegar
3 tablespoons (45 ml) Worcestershire sauce

HARISSA HABANERO BUTTER
1 cup (225 g) unsalted butter, at room temperature
2 habanero peppers, seeded and diced
2 shallots, diced
2 tablespoons (32 g) *Smoky Southwest Harissa* (page 42)
Zest of 1 lime
Juice of 1 lime
1 teaspoon kosher salt, plus more as needed

INSTRUCTIONS

Heat the smoker up to 250°F (120°C). Rub the pork steaks with a thin coat of yellow mustard as a binder. Season all sides generously with as much *Brad's Smoke Rub* as needed.

Place the pork steaks on the smoker and allow them to cook undisturbed for 90 minutes.

Prepare the basting sauce by boiling the water in a small saucepan. Add the shallots and boil for 6–8 minutes until they are soft. Remove from the heat and stir in the butter, apple cider vinegar, and Worcestershire sauce. Keep the pot on low heat or transfer to the smoker.

Start basting the pork steaks after the first 90 minutes and every 45 minutes after that. Continue this for the next 3–4 hours until the pork is about 185°F (85°C). The meat will be tender to the touch, practically falling off the bone if you tugged at it with a fork.

Make the compound butter while the pork is smoking. Melt 2 tablespoons (28 g) of the butter in a skillet over medium-low heat. Add the habanero peppers and shallots to the pan and cook for 3–4 minutes until they start to soften. Remove the pan from the heat and allow it to cool to room temperature. Pour the mix into a food processor along with the remaining 6 tablespoons (85 g) of room-temperature butter, *Smoky Southwest Harissa*, lime zest, lime juice, and salt. Purée until the butter is smooth, taste, and adjust with salt as needed. Place in the fridge until ready to use.

Remove the pork steaks and allow them to rest for about 30 minutes before serving. Top the steaks with the *Harissa Habanero Butter* and let the flavors melt in.

NOTE: You'll need thicker cuts of steak for this recipe, so don't skimp on size. Local butchers should be able to prepare these for you; otherwise, you can purchase a pork shoulder and ask them to slice it. There's a thick bone in the center, so don't try this at home without proper equipment.

ANCHO-ORANGE
PULLED PORK

SERVES
12
PEOPLE

Chile and citrus combinations from around the world often inspire my barbecue. *Chilorio* is a traditional dish from the state of Sinaloa in Mexico, comprising slow-simmered pork that is fried and then cooked in a chile sauce, which was used as a means to preserve the meat before refrigeration. Used in tacos, burritos, and tortas, this recipe has the flexibility of American-style smoked pulled pork. While this recipe is inspired by chilorio, I have evolved it over time. The flavors are similar, but the technique is different. The pork shoulder is slowly smoked until tender enough to shred before being massaged with a rich sauce of chiles, orange juice, and spices. I like doing this because you're sure to achieve deep flavor that seasons every bite. The only challenging part is choosing between a taco or a sandwich for the pork when it's done.

1 bone-in pork butt, about 8 pounds (3.6 kg)
½ cup (70 g) *Brad's Smoke Rub* (page 34)

ANCHO-ORANGE SAUCE
5 dried ancho chiles
3 dried guajillo chiles
½ cup (120 ml) fresh orange juice
Juice of 1 lime
⅓ cup (80 ml) apple cider vinegar
3 garlic cloves
½ teaspoon ground cumin
1 teaspoon dried Mexican oregano
1 teaspoon white sugar
1 teaspoon kosher salt, plus more as needed

SPRITZ
½ cup (120 ml) apple cider vinegar
¼ cup (60 ml) fresh orange juice

FOR SERVING
12–16 6–8 inch (15-20 cm) flour tortillas, warmed
2–3 avocados, sliced
1 cup (224 g) *Hot Pickled Red Onions* (page 48)

EQUIPMENT
Spray bottle

INSTRUCTIONS
Prep the pork butt by first removing the skin, if any. Season the pork with an even layer of *Brad's Smoke Rub*. Allow the rub to set into the pork for 30–40 minutes.

Preheat the smoker to 265°F (129°C). Once at temperature, place the pork butt inside, fat cap facing up. Leave the pork undisturbed for about 3 hours.

Prepare the sauce. Clean the chiles with a damp paper towel. Heat a cast iron skillet over medium-high heat and toast the chiles, flipping occasionally, until puffed and lightly browned for 4–5 minutes. Place them in a large bowl and pour hot water over them, allowing them to hydrate for about 20 minutes. Remove the chiles and place them in a blender with the rest of the sauce ingredients. Purée to a smooth sauce, taste, and adjust with salt as needed. Pour into a container and if making ahead of time, place in the fridge while the pork continues to cook.

Mix and apple cider vinegar and orange juice in a spray bottle. ➤➤

above Shredding the pork before adding the sauce ensures you'll get the best coverage.

After the first 3 hours, open the smoker and spritz the outside with the vinegar–orange juice mix. Continue to cook the pork butt at the same temperature for another 5 hours, spritzing every hour or more as needed. The pork will visibly shrink, and the fat cap will eventually start to crack and split as the 8-hour mark approaches.

Roll out 2 large sheets of heavy-duty aluminum foil, 3–4 times as long as the widest side of the pork butt. Place the foil on your workstation, overlapping the two sheets, with the shiny side facing up. Spritz the pork butt one last time before wrapping. Tightly roll the pork butt in the foil, folding in the sides as you roll to ensure it is completely sealed. Continue to roll and fold in the sides, gently patting the foil to make sure there are no air pockets inside.

Place the foil-wrapped pork back into the smoker and continue to cook for another 2 hours or until the pork registers just over 200°F (93°C) internal temperature. Remove the pork when ready and allow it to rest while wrapped at room temperature for about an hour before shredding.

Remove the bone and shred the pork. Warm up the *Ancho-Orange Sauce* if needed and pour it onto the pork and mix with your hands, seasoning the pulled pork.

Serve with warm tortillas, avocados, and *Hot Pickled Red Onions*.

GRILLED PORK TENDERLOIN
AL PASTOR

Eating this plate of pork and chiles is truly an experience, taking your mouth on a journey from heat to sweet. The bright red color from the marinated pork is a signal for you to stop and take a bite. It's not as spicy as it looks. In fact, the flavors of *al pastor* are quite fruity. Dried chiles are toasted and blended with a mix of aromatics and citrus to create an incredibly vibrant marinade. Grilling the pork directly over the coals enhances those flavors, transforming over the fire with caramelized chiles. This dish is rounded out with a simple *Pineapple Salsa* for fresh flavors and texture. Try this recipe and experiment by using the sauce with other meats such as grilled shrimp or chicken.

AL PASTOR MARINADE
4 dried chile de árbol peppers
5 dried guajillo chilies
½ cup (120 ml) fresh orange juice
Juice of 1 lime
⅓ cup (80 ml) distilled white vinegar
1 teaspoon dried Mexican oregano
1 tablespoon (16 g) achiote paste
3 garlic cloves, peeled
1 teaspoon white sugar
2 teaspoons kosher salt

PORK
2 pork tenderloins, 12–14 ounces
   (340–390 g) each

AVOCADO SERRANO CREMA
1 serrano chile
3 tablespoons (45 ml) fresh lime juice
2 scallions, chopped
¼ cup (60 g) sour cream
2 avocados, quartered
¼ cup (4 g) chopped fresh cilantro
Kosher salt

PINEAPPLE SALSA
3 cups (465 g) diced fresh pineapple
½ cup (80 g) diced red onion
¼ cup (4 g) chopped fresh cilantro
3 tablespoons (45 ml) fresh lime juice
1 jalapeño pepper, diced
Kosher salt and black pepper

INSTRUCTIONS
Prepare the marinade. Clean the chiles with damp paper towel. Heat a cast iron skillet over medium-high heat and toast the chiles for about 4–5 minutes, flipping occasionally, until puffed and lightly browned. Place them in a large bowl and pour hot water over them, allowing them to hydrate for about 20 minutes. Discard the seeds and stems and add the chiles to a blender with the rest of the marinade ingredients. Purée until completely smooth, taste, and adjust if needed.

Trim the pork tenderloins to remove any silver skin on the outside. Place them in a large resealable plastic bag. Pour the *Al Pastor Marinade* into the bag, moving the tenderloins around to ensure they are completely coated. Marinate in the fridge for at least 4 hours, ideally overnight. ➤

Prepare the crema and salsa while the pork is soaking up flavors. For the crema, start by chopping the serrano chile (remove seeds and membrane if too spicy) and place into a blender. Pour in the lime juice and allow the serrano to soak. While you prep the rest of the ingredients. Add the scallions, sour cream, avocados, and cilantro with a pinch of salt and purée until completely smooth. Taste and adjust if needed. Place in the fridge until ready to use.

In a large bowl, mix together all the salsa the ingredients. This should be prepared ahead of time and placed in the fridge to allow the flavors to meld together before it's time to serve.

Preheat the grill for direct cooking at medium-high heat, 350–400°F (180–200°C). Clean the grill grates and oil them as needed.

Remove the pork from the resealable bag and wipe off any excess marinade. Place the pork on the hot grill. Cook the tenderloins, flipping about every 90 seconds. Continue to sear and flip, building a crust that will give off aromas of roasted chiles. Grill the pork until the internal temperature reads about 135°F (57°C), which should take 6–8 minutes. Pull the tenderloins from the grill and allow to rest on a cutting board, tented with aluminum foil, for about 10 minutes.

Slice and serve with the spicy *Avocado Serrano Crema* and fresh *Pineapple Salsa*.

SMOKED CHORIZO
MEATBALLS

One of my favorite dishes that my wife prepares is *albóndigas*, a Mexican meatball soup. She transforms the typically clear broth into a thicker, spicier version packed with fresh chipotles and tomatoes. We eventually took this idea to the grill to create smoked meatballs with a savory, spicy sauce. The combination of beef and spicy pork chorizo creates an incredibly juicy, savory meatball with a pop of herbs from the mint and cilantro. A skillet of sauce is cooked alongside the meatballs, bathing them at the end to incorporate all of the flavors. Serve these over freshly cooked pasta, rice, of pile them into an incredible *Roasted Chile Meatball Hero* (page 133).

SMOKED TOMATO SAUCE

3 tablespoons (45 g) chipotle chiles in adobo
½ white onion, diced
4 garlic cloves, peeled
1 can (28 ounces, or 785 g) fire-roasted tomatoes
1 teaspoon smoked paprika
½ cup (120 ml) beef broth
Kosher salt

CHORIZO MEATBALLS

1 pound (455 g) ground beef, 90/10 preferred
1 pound (455 g) pork chorizo
2 large eggs
½ white onion, grated
½ cup (56 g) panko breadcrumbs
¼ cup (24 g) chopped fresh mint
¼ cup (4 g) chopped fresh cilantro
2 tablespoons (6 g) dried Mexican oregano
1 teaspoon kosher salt
1 teaspoon ground cumin
½ teaspoon black pepper

FOR GARNISH

½ cup (8 g) chopped fresh cilantro

INSTRUCTIONS

Prepare the smoker for indirect cooking at 350°F (180°C).

Prepare the sauce. Place the chipotle chiles, onion, and garlic into a blender and blitz to break up the chiles as much as possible. Add the rest of the sauce ingredients and purée until the desired consistency. Taste and adjust. Pour the sauce into a large cast iron skillet or grill-safe pan.

In a large, chilled bowl, combine the ingredients for the meatballs. Using your hands, mix all of the ingredients until evenly combined. Taste test the mixture by cooking a small sample in a frying pan on the stove until cooked through. Adjust

the seasoning if needed. Roll the meat into 1½-inch (3.8 cm) balls and place on a parchment-lined baking sheet, leaving space between each meatball.

Place the meatball tray and the skillet with the sauce in the smoker, allowing them to cook for about 25 minutes.

Once the meatballs have hit 135–140°F (57–60°C) internal temperature, transfer them to the skillet with the *Smoked Tomato Sauce*, nestling them in. Continue to cook until the meatballs have reached 165°F (74°C), which should take another 10 minutes or so.

Sprinkle the chopped cilantro over the top.

ROASTED CHILE
MEATBALL HERO

SERVES
ABOUT

4

PEOPLE

Growing up, if we were ever to stop at a sandwich shop, I'd always go for the meatball hero. High-quality meatballs and sauce, toasted bread, and copious amounts of melty cheese are requirements for this simple, but epic sandwich. The *Smoked Chorizo Meatballs* (page 130) transform the classic flavors into something new, topped with salty and melty cheeses and *Pickled Jalapeños* for an explosion of flavors. Feel free to use the classic combination of Parmesan and mozzarella if you don't have access to the Mexican cheeses. Just don't burn that bread—the roasting happens fast.

INGREDIENTS
1 batch *Smoked Chorizo Meatballs*
   (page 130)
4 hoagie rolls, or individual-size
   Italian-style rolls
¼ cup (30 g) Cotija cheese, or (25 g)
   freshly grated Parmesan cheese
1 pound (455 g) shredded Oaxaca
   cheese, or Monterey Jack
Pickled Jalapeños (page 46)

INSTRUCTIONS
Preheat the grill or oven to 450°F (230°C, or gas mark 8).

Make sure the meatballs and sauce are warmed all the way through. Heat them in a pot or skillet over medium heat if needed.

Slice the rolls down the middle but not all the way through. Open them up and place on a baking sheet. Spoon about ½ cup (120 ml) of the sauce onto the inside of each roll. Layer 4–5 meatballs into the roll and top with the salty Cotija cheese, then the Oaxaca cheese.

Bake the meatball heroes for 6–8 minutes or until the bread is toasty. Remove from the grill or oven and top with *Pickled Jalapeños*, if desired. Serve immediately. Bite with caution— those heroes are hot!

CHILE VERDE
BABY BACK RIBS

SERVES

8–10
PEOPLE

Serve me a big bowl of pork chile verde with a side of fresh tortillas and I'll be your friend forever. The thick stew of fresh tomatillos, herbs, and chiles provides a vibrant, complex flavor to the tender pork. I've spent years working out different variations of this for the smoker, and these ribs just hit right. A slow smoke bath for the first half creates an amazing bark, layering in the spices and textures. My favorite moment is opening the smoker right after glazing the ribs with the bright green chile verde sauce—the smells are incredible. Each bite is deeply flavored and succulent, picking up the charred jalapeños and poblanos. Inspired by the traditional dish of *chicharrones en salsa verde*, these ribs are finished with crispy bits of crushed-up pork rinds to add texture. Make sure you have some friends or family with you because this recipe makes plenty for all.

4 racks baby back ribs, 1½–2 pounds
(680–900 g) each
2 cups (276 g) *Brad's Smoke Rub*
(page 34)

CHILE VERDE BBQ SAUCE
1 poblano chile
1 jalapeño pepper
2 pounds (900 g) tomatillos, washed
and quartered
1 garlic clove, peeled
1 cup (235 ml) distilled white vinegar
¼ cup (60 ml) water
½ cup (80 g) medium dice white onion
½ cup (115 g) brown sugar
½ teaspoon ground cumin
½ teaspoon mustard powder
1 teaspoon kosher salt

SPRITZ
1 cup (235 ml) apple cider vinegar

FOR SERVING
2 cups (160 g) pork rinds, crushed

EQUIPMENT
Spray bottle

INSTRUCTIONS
Prepare the smoker for indirect cooking at 250°F (120°C). Use a mild hardwood such as apple or oak.

Start by trimming the ribs. Place a rack on the cutting board with the bone-side facing up. Trim the excess skirt meat attached to the membrane. You may also remove the membrane, which is the thick silver skin covering the bones. Using a butter knife, stick it between the membrane and a bone and gently pry it up.

A paper towel provides the best grip for ripping it off.

Season the rack of ribs with about ½ cup (70 g) of *Brad's Smoke Rub* per rack, making sure to coat both sides evenly.

Place the racks of ribs on the smoker, bone-side down. Allow them to cook for an hour undisturbed.

Prepare the BBQ sauce. Heat up the grill or a gas burner to char the chiles. Char the poblano chile and jalapeño pepper until the skin is blistering and burnt and then place them in a plastic bag, allowing them to steam for a few minutes. Once cool, discard the stems and seeds. Set aside. ➽

Combine the rest of the sauce ingredients in a large saucepan. Heat the pan on the stove over high heat, bringing it to a boil. Once the liquid starts to boil, reduce the heat to medium and cook for about 20 minutes. Stir often, as the tomatillos will release a lot of liquid.

Once the tomatillos have broken down, remove the pan from the heat. Pour all the contents into a large mesh strainer, draining any excess liquid. Transfer the solids into a blender with the roasted poblano and jalapeño and purée until smooth. Pour into a heatproof container and set aside.

Check on the ribs after the first hour. Fill a spray bottle with the vinegar and spritz the edges of the ribs with it. This will keep them moist and lessen the chances of burning. Do this every 45–60 minutes. Allow the ribs to smoke for 90 more minutes.

After the first 2½ hours of smoking have passed, it's time to wrap the ribs. Spritz the ribs a final time and transfer one of the racks to a sheet of heavy-duty aluminum foil, placing meat-side down.

Check to make sure there are no large bones poking out that could rip the foil. Wrap up the meat tightly, with the seam on the top. Place this rack back on the smoker, with the meat-side facing down. Repeat for the rest of the ribs. Cook for 1 hour at the same temperature, about 250°F (120°C).

After the final stretch, open the foil and check the ribs. Feel for the ribs in the middle to see if they are tender and pliable. There should be a slight bend when picking it up in the middle. Remove them from the foil and set them on the grates, bone-side down. Brush the *Chile Verde BBQ Sauce* on the ribs and cook for 10–15 minutes further to set the sauce. Remove the ribs from the smoker and allow them to rest, tented in loose foil, for 20–30 minutes before slicing. Sprinkle with the pork rinds and serve.

CHIPOTLE PORK BELLY
BURNT ENDS
WITH JALAPEÑO BERRY SAUCE

MAKES
ABOUT

5
POUNDS
(2.3 KG)

Pork belly burnt ends are a staple for many barbecue lovers. They're incredibly juicy, crispy from the bark, and able to soak up any flavor you can imagine. This pork belly is seasoned with a gentle touch of chipotle, which is mellowed out by the brown sugar and spices. I was inspired by Dorie Greenspan, in a cooking class where she explained how to use marionberries with soy sauce and ginger to make an incredible umami-based sauce. The jalapeños, ginger, and blueberries create the wild flavor in this one, fortified with a touch of salt and garlic. Adding wildflower honey is the secret. It's a subtle floral flavor to bridge the worlds of barbecue and the savory sauce. Serve these sweet, porky bites to the masses or just make them for dessert. There's no judgment here.

1 pork belly, 5–6 pounds
   (2.3–2.7 kg), skin removed
¾ cup (170 g) brown sugar
¼ cup (28 g) smoked paprika
3 tablespoons (54 g) salt
2 teaspoons black pepper
1 tablespoon (8 g) chipotle chile
   powder
1 tablespoon (9 g) garlic powder
2 tablespoons (22 g) yellow mustard
½ cup (120 ml) apple juice
3 tablespoons (60 g) wildflower honey

JALAPEÑO BERRY SAUCE
2 cups (290 g) fresh blueberries
1 jalapeño pepper, diced
½ teaspoon chopped fresh ginger
3 tablespoons (60 g) wildflower
   honey
2 garlic cloves, roughly chopped
½ teaspoon chipotle chile powder

2 tablespoons (28 ml) soy sauce
½ teaspoon kosher salt
3 tablespoons (39 g) white sugar
1 teaspoon distilled white vinegar

INSTRUCTIONS
Prepare the smoker for indirect cooking at 250°F (120°C).

Slice the pork belly into 2-inch (5 cm) cubes. Mix the brown sugar, paprika, salt, pepper, chipotle chile powder, and garlic powder together in a small bowl. Rub the cubes of pork belly with a light coat of the yellow mustard. Season the pork generously on all sides with the seasoning blend. Place the pork belly onto a large wire rack or jerky rack. Smoke the pork for about 3 hours, undisturbed.

Prepare the sauce. Place all of the sauce ingredients except the vinegar into a medium-size saucepan over medium heat. Once it just boils, lower the heat to a simmer. Cook for 25–30 minutes, stirring frequently. The berries will break down, and the jalapeño pepper will completely soften. Allow it to cool slightly and purée the sauce in a blender until completely smooth. Stir in the vinegar, taste, and adjust if needed.

After 3 hours of smoking time, set out two large sheets of heavy-duty aluminum foil. Remove the pork from the smoker and spread half of it out on each piece of the foil in a single layer. Pour half of the apple juice in the center of each. Wrap the foil very tightly around the pork, ➥

with the seam completely closed at the top. Use a double-layer if you need to. Place the foil pouches back onto the smoker, with the temperature increased to 300°F (150°C). Cook for another 45 minutes and then check. The pork cubes should be extremely tender with an internal temperature around 205°F (96°C).

Carefully open the foil packets. Divide the *Jalapeño Berry Sauce* and honey between the two packets, pouring over the pork. Gently toss the pork to coat, leave the foil packets open, and return to the smoker for another 15–20 minutes to caramelize the sauce.

Remove the pork from the smoker and dig in.

NOTE: You can prepare the sauce ahead of time. It will be fresh for just about 2 weeks in the fridge. Get adventurous and explore different combinations of chiles and berries for the sauce. When cooking with berries that have notable seeds, such as strawberries, blackberries, or raspberries, you will want to finish the sauce through a fine-mesh strainer to get rid of the seeds. One of my favorite alternatives is a combination of fresh raspberries and serrano chiles.

HALIBUT, SCALLOPS, SHRIMP, SALMON & MORE

CORN HUSK-WRAPPED
HALIBUT
WITH JALAPEÑO BASIL BUTTER

<table>
<tr><td>SERVES
4–6
PEOPLE</td></tr>
</table>

One of the first dishes my wife cooked for me was fish *en papillote*, a simple preparation of baking fish in parchment paper with herbs and vegetables. Taking this technique to the grill would burn the parchment paper, but thankfully, there are other alternatives. For example, removing an ear of corn from the husk provides a perfect package for halibut. The corn can be grilled on the side, along with other vegetables, to create a delicious grilled corn salad. Bitter jalapeños are paired with fresh basil and a touch of lemon to create a wonderful compound butter for the fish and the grilled vegetables.

JALAPEÑO BASIL BUTTER

1 jalapeño pepper, seeded and diced
1 cup (225 g) unsalted butter, at room temperature
¼ cup (10 g) fresh basil, chopped
Zest of 1 lemon
½ teaspoon kosher salt

CORN HUSK-WRAPPED HALIBUT

4 ears fresh corn, with husks
Cotton string, about 8 pieces cut at 6 inches (15 cm) in length
4 halibut fillets, about 6 ounces (170 g) each, skin removed
1 teaspoon kosher salt
1 teaspoon black pepper
¼ cup (80 g) *Jalapeño Basil Butter*, at room temperature

GRILLED CORN SALAD

¼ cup (80 g) *Jalapeño Basil Butter*, at room temperature
1 cup (200 g) diced *Pickled Sweet Bell Peppers* (page 45)
2 scallions, chopped
1 teaspoon paprika
Juice of 1 lemon
Salt

INSTRUCTIONS

Prepare the compound butter. Mix the jalapeño pepper, butter, basil, lemon zest, and salt together in a food processor until combined. Taste and adjust. Set aside, keeping at room temperature unless made ahead of time.

Pull back the husks from each ear of corn carefully, keeping it attached at the base. Remove all of the corn silk and snap off the ear of corn. Place the husks attached to the stem in a large pot of water to soak for 30 minutes. Also add the cotton string pieces to soak, which will prevent them from burning on the grill.

Remove the husks and string from the water, shaking the husks dry. Season the halibut fillets with salt and pepper and place one piece inside each husk. Smear 1 tablespoon (20 g) of the *Jalapeño Basil Butter* on the top of each fillet and carefully close up the husks. Tie the top of the husks with a piece of the wet cotton string. Use a second piece in the middle of the husks if needed to keep it closed.

Prepare the grill for a 2-zone cooking setup at medium heat, 300–350°F (150–180°C), with the hot coals on one side. ➤➤

Clean the grill grates and oil them as needed.

Place the ears of corn and wrapped corn husks on the grill directly above the coals. Allow the corn husks to cook for about 5 minutes before flipping. Continue to cook this way, flipping twice more in 5 minute intervals. Turn the corn often to make sure all sides have a nice char.

Check the halibut with a temperature probe, carefully piercing into the top. The fish should be at 125–130°F (49–54°C) internal temperature. Remove when ready and leave it wrapped to rest for a few minutes.

Remove the corn when cooked. Carefully cut the kernels off the cob and place into a bowl with a few tablespoons (60–80 g) of the *Jalapeño Basil Butter*, to taste. Add the *Pickled Sweet Bell Peppers*, scallions, paprika, lemon, and salt. Mix the corn salad and taste, adjusting seasoning as needed.

Open up each corn husk and spoon some of the *Grilled Corn Salad* next to the halibut. Serve immediately while warm.

SUMMER BBQ GRILLED
SCALLOPS AND CORN

SERVES
4–5
PEOPLE

Grilling in the summertime reminds me of basting food with barbecue sauce, piles of grilled corn, and lots of bright citrus slices. Summer recipes are typically simpler to prepare and quicker to cook, as everyone is looking forward to kicking back and relaxing. Scallops are incredible right off the grill, seared quickly to caramelize the outside while adding a bit of char. They absorb flavors very well, and brushing them with the barbecue butter adds just enough seasoning without overwhelming their natural taste. If you haven't tried scallops or are intimidated by them, this is the recipe for you. I recommend using a spicy barbecue sauce for the compound butter, which counters the naturally sweet flavors.

2 pounds (900 g) jumbo scallops
⅓ cup (85 g) *Nashville Hot BBQ Sauce* (page 95)
¼ cup (55 g) unsalted butter
4 ears of corn, shucked
2 tablespoons (28 ml) olive oil
Kosher salt and black pepper

FOR GARNISH
¼ cup (15 g) chopped fresh parsley
Lemon slices
Kosher salt

INSTRUCTIONS

Preheat the grill for direct cooking at high heat.

Take the scallops out of their packaging and pat them dry with a paper towel. Place them on a wire rack in the fridge until ready to cook. Do not season them ahead of time.

Melt the *Nashville Hot BBQ Sauce* and butter together in a small saucepan until they combine.

Place the corn on the grill and cook, turning often. Closing the lid between flips will help the corn cook a little faster. Once the corn starts to char, baste it lightly with the BBQ butter and continue to flip. The corn will be ready after about 10 minutes total. Set the corn on a plate covered lightly with aluminum foil while the scallops cook.

Remove the scallops from the fridge and place them on a tray. Lightly drizzle with olive oil, coating the scallops on all sides. Season with salt and pepper on all sides as well.

Make sure your grill grates are very clean and lightly oil them if you can. Clean, slick grates help the scallops cook properly without sticking. ➤➤

Grill the scallops directly over the coals for about 3 minutes and carefully flip with a thin spatula (avoid using tongs). They should easily release from the grill grates. Brush the scallops with the BBQ butter and cook for another 2–3 minutes. Flip one last time, baste again with the BBQ butter, and then remove the scallops from the grill. The internal temperature should be 115–120°F (46–49°C), which will continue to cook as you take them off the grill.

Shave the corn off the cobs and serve with the grilled scallops, garnished with chopped parsley and lemon slices. Season to taste.

HALIBUT, SCALLOPS, SHRIMP, SALMON & MORE

HULI HULI SHRIMP,
SHISHITO, AND PINEAPPLE SKEWERS

These skewers take full advantage of the Japanese shishito peppers, pairing them with sweet pineapple and shrimp, glazed with a rich huli huli sauce. The balance of bitter, spicy, and sweet is greater than the sum of its parts. Everything cooks evenly and quickly, making this a convenient, flavorful weeknight meal. Serve these skewers on their own as an appetizer or make them a meal with some delicious steamed rice.

SHRIMP MARINADE
2 tablespoons (28 ml) canola oil
3 tablespoons (3 g) chopped fresh
    cilantro
1 jalapeño pepper, seeded and diced
2 tablespoons (28 ml) fresh lime juice
1 teaspoon kosher salt

SKEWERS
1 pound (455 g) large shrimp,
    16/20 count, peeled and deveined
16 shishito peppers
2 cups (330 g) fresh pineapple, cut
    into 1-inch (2.5 cm) cubes

SPICY HULI HULI SAUCE
1 cup (235 ml) pineapple juice
2 tablespoons (30 g) brown sugar
2 tablespoons (28 ml) soy sauce
2 tablespoons (30 g) ketchup
2 tablespoons (28 ml) sherry vinegar
1 tablespoon (4 g) red pepper flakes
1 tablespoon (10 g) minced garlic

½ tablespoon grated fresh ginger
1 teaspoon sesame oil

EQUIPMENT
Grilling skewers (metal or wooden)

INSTRUCTIONS
Preheat the grill for direct cooking at medium-high heat, 350–400°F (180–200°C). Clean the grill grates and oil them as needed.

In a small bowl, mix together the ingredients for the quick marinade. Prepare the shrimp, making sure they are cleaned properly. Place them in a sealed container or zipped bag and pour the marinade over, making sure the shrimp are completely coated. Make sure to reserve some of the marinade for serving. Refrigerate for 30 to 45 minutes.

Prepare the skewers. Drain the marinade from the shrimp and lightly pat them dry with paper towels. Thread a shrimp onto the skewer, piercing twice to secure it in place. Add a shishito pepper and then a pineapple cube. Keep alternating between the ingredients until there are 4–5 skewers ready for the grill.

Prepare the sauce. In a medium-size bowl, mix all sauce ingredients and taste and adjust.

Place the skewers on the grill directly above the coals and allow them to sear for 2–3 minutes. Flip and glaze the top with the sauce. Cook for another 2–3 minutes and flip again, glazing the second side. Repeat the process one last time and cook until the shrimp are done, about 120°F (49°C) internal temperature.

The skewers are done when the shrimp are opaque and start to firm up, the shishitos are blistered, and the pineapple has some char.

Serve immediately with the reserved *Spicy Huli Huli Sauce* as desired.

NOTE: Metal kebab skewers work best for this recipe, as the flat blade will prevent the ingredients from spinning around while flipping on the grill. If you don't have those, use two wooden skewers side by side to keep everything in place.

If you're using wooden skewers, soak them in water for at least 30 minutes in advance to prevent them from burning when cooking on the grill.

HATCH CHILE SMOKED
SHRIMP SKILLET

It's hard to imagine that a giant pan of shrimp, gently bathed in garlic butter, could be improved upon. It turns out that buttery Hatch chiles are the perfect ingredient to spice things up though. Cooking this recipe couldn't be easier, as you really don't have to do much more than melt butter and mix everything in the pan. The combination of a lower smoking temperature and melted butter keeps the shrimp extremely moist. There will be plenty of buttery chile sauce, so make sure you have some crusty bread on hand to soak up all of the juices. Feel free to swap out the chiles and try different combinations, such as roasted poblanos or diced chipotles in adobo.

INGREDIENTS

2 pounds (900 g) large shrimp, peeled and deveined

2 teaspoons *Light Chili Powder* (page 31)

2 sticks (1 cup, or 225 g) salted butter

4 garlic cloves, minced

½ cup (90 g) roasted and diced Hatch chiles

Crusty French bread for serving

Juice of 1 lime

¼ cup (4 g) chopped fresh cilantro

INSTRUCTIONS

Prepare the smoker or grill for indirect cooking at 275°F (140°C). The shrimp don't smoke very long, so you can use a stronger wood flavor such as mesquite or pecan if you'd prefer. If using a grill, prepare a 2-zone cooking setup, with the hot coals on one side.

Pat the shrimp dry and make sure they are cleaned and ready to be cooked. Place the shrimp in a large bowl and season with the *Light Chili Powder*, tossing to coat. Gently melt the butter in a saucepan over medium heat. Remove from the heat when melted and add the garlic and Hatch chiles, stirring to incorporate.

Place the shrimp into a large skillet, making sure they lay flat in the pan. You may also use a large aluminum pan or baking dish. Pour the butter sauce evenly over all of the shrimp to ensure they are coated.

Smoke the shrimp for 20–30 minutes, depending on the size of your shrimp. They will turn an orangish color and should reach 120°F (49°C) internal temperature. Remove from the grill and toast up some slices of the crusty bread. Squeeze the lime juice over the shrimp and top with chopped cilantro. Serve immediately and don't forget to dip that crusty bread in the sauce!

NOTE: Togarashi is a traditional Japanese seasoning used with rice, noodles, and many more dishes. If you do not have access to this, use 2 tablespoons (10 g) of toasted sesame seeds, red pepper flakes, and crumble 1/2 sheet of toasted nori (seaweed sheets) to make a simplified version. Don't skip it though. This topping adds salt, umami, and texture to an otherwise soft dish.

"CALIFORNIA ROLL"
CRAB-STUFFED AVOCADOS

SERVES
6–8
PEOPLE

Everyone starts somewhere on their food journey, and the classic California sushi roll happened to be one of my first breakouts from the typical meal. I had discovered this combination of stuffing the seasoned crab into an avocado years before I met my wife, creating a healthier meal packed with protein. Wondering if it could be smoked (spoiler: yes), the generously stuffed avocado was bathed with mesquite for a short period of time. Grilling the avocados enhances their natural flavors, also making them sweeter. Smoking the spicy crab briefly adds just enough wood-fired flavor without overwhelming the naturally briny flavors. Top these with additional sriracha hot sauce and a generous sprinkle of crunchy togarashi.

2 cups lump crabmeat, about 16 ounces
   (455 g)
2 scallions, chopped
¾ cup diced English cucumber,
   ¼-inch (6 mm) cubes
2 tablespoons (28 ml) sriracha hot
   sauce, plus more as needed
½ cup (115 g) *Smoked Garlic Aioli*
   (page 37) or mayonnaise
½ teaspoon sea salt
4 medium-size avocados
2 tablespoons (28 ml) canola oil

FOR GARNISH
Sriracha hot sauce
2–3 tablespoons (12–18 g) togarashi
Soy sauce

INSTRUCTIONS

Prepare the grill for a 2-zone cooking setup at medium heat, 300–350°F (150–180°C), with the hot coals on one side. Clean the grates well to ensure the avocado doesn't stick.

In a large bowl, mix together the crab, scallions, cucumber, sriracha, *Smoked Garlic Aioli*, and salt. Taste and adjust as needed. Be aware that the crab has a natural saltiness and will be garnished with soy sauce and togarashi, which both have added sodium.

Slice the avocados in half, remove the pit, and brush lightly with oil. Place the avocados on the grill facedown directly over the coals. Cook for 2–3 minutes until grill marks have formed and then remove.

Stuff each half of the avocado with the crab filling, which should be piled fairly high. Place each half of crab-stuffed avocado carefully on the cooler side of the grill, away from the coals. Add some wood chips if desired for extra smoke flavor. Cook for about 15 minutes until the crab has taken on some smoke color and warmed through.

Carefully remove from the grill with tongs. Serve immediately with a garnish of sriracha and a dash of togarashi for a crispy topping and soy sauce on the side.

TANDOORI
GRILLED LOBSTER
WITH LEMON PARSLEY AIOLI

Naturally sweet lobster typically doesn't call for more than butter and garlic, but this tandoori-inspired spice blend is worth trying. Lobster tails over the fire smell incredible, especially basted with herbs and bold chiles. Searing lobster at high heat with the shell creates this roasted, caramelized flavor. This tandoori glaze borrows the spices from *Tandoori Butterflied Chicken Drumsticks* (page 101), transforming it into a bold baste for the lobster. Pairing with a simple sauce mixed with lemon and herbs tempers the spicy flavors while additionally seasoning the lobster.

TANDOORI GLAZE

4 tablespoons (60 ml) canola oil, plus more as needed
1 tablespoon (8 g) guajillo chile powder
2 tablespoons (16 g) grated fresh ginger
2 tablespoons (20 g) grated garlic
1 teaspoon ground cumin
1 teaspoon ground coriander
1 teaspoon paprika
1 teaspoon kosher salt

LEMON PARSLEY AIOLI

⅔ cup (150 g) *Smoked Garlic Aioli* (page 37)
1 tablespoon (6 g) lemon zest
¼ cup (60 ml) fresh lemon juice, plus more as needed
2 teaspoons Dijon mustard
½ cup (30 g) chopped fresh flat-leaf parsley
Salt

4 lobster tails, split in half lengthwise and cleaned

INSTRUCTIONS

Prepare the glaze by warming the oil in a small saucepan over medium heat. Add the rest of the glaze ingredients and whisk to incorporate. If the mix is too thick, add a little more oil to thin it out. The spices will bloom, giving off a strong aromatic smell. After a few minutes, remove from the heat and allow to cool.

Prepare the aioli. Whisk all the aioli ingredients together in a small bowl. Taste and adjust with salt or additional lemon juice as needed.

Preheat the grill for direct cooking at medium heat, 350–400°F (180–200°C). Clean the grill grates and oil them as needed.

Brush each half of the lobster tail generously with the *Tandoori Glaze*.

Grill the lobster tails. Place them on the grill with the meat facing down toward the heat and cook for 2–3 minutes. Flip the lobster tails over and brush again with the glaze. Cook for another 2–3 minutes until just cooked through. The internal temperature should be 135–140°F (57–60°C) and the color of the meat should be a creamy white throughout.

The lobster will cool quickly, so feel free to serve immediately with a side of the *Lemon Parsley Aioli*.

NOTE: This recipe works well for smaller pieces of salmon too, just focus on the timing and temperature. Try this sauce with other meats such as chicken, pork, or even lamb.

PLANKED
POMEGRANATE HARISSA
SALMON

Every time I think about salmon on the grill, the first thing that pops into my head are cedar grilling planks. They are so easy to use, yet they add an amazing wood-fired flavor that pairs well with chiles. This is one of those meals you can make at the last minute, picking up some salmon at the store on your way home and mixing a few things together for the sauce. Combining the smoky harissa with sweet citrus and tart pomegranate creates a bold glaze that pairs well with lighter flavors. Paint it on your salmon for this recipe and toss it in the grill. I'd recommend serving with *Lemon-Serrano Grilled Summer Squash* (page 175).

¼ cup (64 g) *Smoky Southwest Harissa* (page 42)

2 tablespoons (28 ml) fresh lemon juice

2 tablespoons (28 ml) olive oil

1 tablespoon (20 g) pomegranate molasses

1 teaspoon kosher salt

1 salmon fillet, about 2 pounds (900 g)

FOR GARNISH

Lemon wedges

Chopped fresh parsley or cilantro (optional)

EQUIPMENT

1 cedar grilling plank, around 5 × 11 inches (13 × 28 cm) soaked in warm water for at least 30 minutes (you may need to add a weight to keep it submerged)

INSTRUCTIONS

Preheat the grill for direct cooking at medium heat, 300–350°F (150–180°C).

In a bowl, mix together the *Smoky Southwest Harissa*, lemon juice, olive oil, pomegranate molasses, and salt. Taste and adjust as needed. Place the salmon in a baking dish and baste the top of it with the glaze. Allow it to marinate while the grill is prepared.

Place the plank on the grill by itself for about 5 minutes. This helps build up a little char flavor before adding the salmon. Place the salmon on the plank, skin-side down. Brush generously with the glaze. Close the lid of the grill for 12–15 minutes. It's better to slightly undercook than overcook, as it will continue to cook while resting.

Remove the salmon from the grill when its internal temperature is 125–130°F (52–54°C) and set the plank on a baking sheet, allowing it to rest for about 5 minutes before serving. Squeeze fresh lemon juice over top and garnish with fresh herbs.

SALADS, SIDES & VEGETABLE MAIN DISHES

DESERT
DEVILED EGGS

Deviled eggs sound like they should pack a punch or at least be spicy. That's not usually the case, but these *Desert Deviled Eggs* deliver. They're spiced with bright red chile paste while also hiding a sting inside for the guests: fresh *Pickled Jalapeños*. *Arizona Adobo Sauce* is mixed with egg yolks, mustard, and butter to create a thick and rich filling, carefully cloaking the surprise jalapeño. *Smoky Bacon Crumble* adds some texture and seasoning, making a well-rounded appetizer.

12 eggs
¼ cup (60 g) mayonnaise, plus more
    as needed
2 tablespoons (28 g) unsalted butter,
    at room temperature
1 tablespoon (15 g) *Arizona Adobo
    Sauce* (page 41)
2 teaspoons Dijon mustard
Kosher salt and black pepper
24 slices *Pickled Jalapeños* (page 46)
Smoky Bacon Crumble (page 165) for
    garnish

INSTRUCTIONS

Fill a saucepan about one-third of the way with cold water. Place the eggs in a single layer at the bottom. Add enough water so that the eggs are covered by 2 inches (5 cm). Place the saucepan on the stove and turn the heat to high, bringing the water to a rolling boil. Once this happens, shut the heat off and place a lid on the saucepan. Allow the eggs to sit in the hot water for 12 minutes.

Carefully remove the eggs from the hot water and place them in a bowl of ice water to cool off, preventing them from overcooking and making them easier to peel. Once cool, take the eggs out of the water and carefully peel the shells. Using a sharp knife, slice them in half with confidence. You don't want shaggy cuts on your deviled eggs. Remove the yolks and place

in a large metal or glass bowl (the adobo can stain plastic).

Add the mayonnaise, butter, *Arizona Adobo Sauce*, Dijon mustard, salt, and pepper to the yolks. Mash the ingredients very well with a fork, making it as smooth as possible. If the filling feels too stiff, you can add a little more mayonnaise until it's the right consistency. Fill a piping bag or a resealable plastic bag with the egg yolk mixture. Cut off the corner of the bag and get ready to pipe the filling into the egg whites.

Set out the egg whites. Place a slice of pickled jalapeño pepper into each of the cavities. Pipe the filling into each of the eggs, hiding the chile. Garnish them with *Smoky Bacon Crumble* and watch the surprised faces of your guests as they bite into their devil-ish egg.

HARISSA
SWEET POTATO SALAD

SERVES

4–6

PEOPLE

Bold main dishes off the grill need an appropriate side dish to complement the flavors. Roasted sweet potatoes with smoky harissa pair perfectly with rich flavors of beef, fire-roasted chicken, and smoky pork. I also reached for dates and pecans (grown locally in Phoenix!) for texture and contrast. Try pairing this dish with *Tandoori Butterflied Chicken Drums* (page 101), *Planked Pomegranate Harissa Salmon* (page 57), or the *Vindaloo-Spiced Lamb Lollipops* (page 85).

SWEET POTATO SALAD

2 pounds (900 g) sweet potatoes, orange variety

4 tablespoons (60 ml) olive oil

¼ teaspoon kosher salt

¼ teaspoon fresh ground black pepper

½ cup (55 g) pecan pieces, optionally toasted

½ cup (89 g) dates, pitted and chopped

4 scallions, finely chopped

HARISSA VINAIGRETTE

2 tablespoons (32 g) *Smoky Southwest Harissa* (page 42)

1 cup (235 ml) canola oil

1 shallot, diced

1 garlic clove

1 tablespoon (20 g) honey

1 tablespoon (15 ml) rice wine vinegar

Juice of 1 lime

¼ teaspoon kosher salt, plus more as needed

INSTRUCTIONS

Preheat the smoker or oven to 425°F (220°C, or gas mark 7). Peel the sweet potatoes and dice them into 1-inch (2.5 cm) pieces. In a large bowl, toss them with the olive oil, salt, and pepper and place on a parchment-lined sheet pan. Make sure they are not crowded together or they will steam instead of roast.

Bake for 25–30 minutes until slightly crispy on the outside. Toss after 10–15 minutes to ensure even cooking.

Add all of the ingredients for the vinaigrette to a blender and purée until smooth. Taste and adjust with salt as needed.

Remove the potatoes from the smoker and allow them to cool. While still slightly warm, toss with the pecans, dates, scallions, and add about ½ cup (120 ml) of *Harissa Vinaigrette* to start. Mix and add more dressing as needed. Serve either still warm or cold.

CREAMY JALAPEÑO POPPER
MAC AND CHEESE

Even when I'm eating a rich, fatty cut of meat, it doesn't turn me away from a big scoop of creamy mac and cheese. I've made many combinations over the years with various cheeses and toppings, but this simple blend stood out when I first made it and has stood the test of time. This mac and cheese has charred jalapeños folded into the sauce, adding to the mild layer of heat from the Pepper Jack. Bitter flavors from the chiles are mellowed out by the rich cheese sauce. Topping the mac and cheese with the *Smoky Bacon Crumble* gives you that wood-fired flavor without having to wait a few hours for it to bake in the smoker. Plus, it's ridiculously creamy.

SMOKY BACON CRUMBLE

½ pound (225 g) bacon
1 tablespoon (8 g) *Light Chili Powder*
    or *Spicy Chili Powder* (page 31)
½ teaspoon black pepper

MAC AND CHEESE

2 jalapeño peppers
1 pound (455 g) elbow macaroni
½ cup (112 g) unsalted butter
¼ cup (31 g) all-purpose flour
2¼ cups (535 ml) whole milk, slightly
    warmed, plus more as needed
8 ounces (225 g) cream cheese, at
    room temperature
2 cups (224 g) shredded Pepper Jack
    cheese
1 cup (120 g) shredded smoked Gouda
    cheese
½ cup (58 g) shredded sharp cheddar
    cheese
1 teaspoon ground mustard
Kosher salt and black pepper

INSTRUCTIONS

Preheat the oven to 400°F (200°C, or gas mark 6). Season the bacon with the chili powder and pepper and bake on a wire rack over a baking sheet for 20 minutes or until extra crispy. Place the bacon on paper towels and pat dry. Once it has cooled completely, break up the bacon into bits for the crumble.

Turn up the oven heat to broil and char the jalapeño peppers on a baking sheet until blistered on all sides and place them in a sealed container for a few minutes to allow the skin to steam. Once the chiles are cooled, discard the skin, stems, and seeds. Dice the jalapeños into small pieces and taste them. This will help you gauge their heat level before stirring them into the sauce later. Personally, I don't remove the seeds.

Bring a large pot of salted water to a boil. Add the elbow macaroni to the water and cook until al dente. Timing may vary based on the pasta itself. Drain the pasta in a strainer to remove excess water when ready.

While the macaroni is cooking, heat a large cast iron skillet over medium heat and melt the butter. Add the flour to the butter and whisk to form a smooth roux. Continue to cook and whisk for 2–3 minutes until the roux is a light-brown color. Slowly pour in the warmed milk while whisking to form a smooth sauce. Make sure the sauce ➤➤

does not boil. It needs to stay at a low simmer. You'll notice the sauce thickening after 3–4 minutes.

Lower your temperature and start to add the cream cheese, a little at a time, gently whisking until it's completely melted before adding more. Do the same for the rest of the cheeses and the ground mustard, whisking and adding a portion at a time until the sauce is melted and smooth. Remove the skillet from the heat.

Stir in the jalapeños and season with salt and pepper to taste. Add the cooked pasta to the cheese sauce and gently stir to coat the macaroni. If the cheese sauce is too thick, add a splash of milk to the skillet and mix it in. Top the mac and cheese with the *Smoky Bacon Crumble* and grab a spoon.

SMOKE AS AN INGREDIENT

It's so tempting to toss just about every dish in the smoker, especially when we have access to pellet grills that can start with a simple push of a button. Rather than overwhelming guests with smoked sides, meats, and desserts, I like to add smoked elements *into* the dishes instead. Using smoked ingredients adds character and complexity to the dishes, creating a balance for the meal.

Some of the most common smoked ingredients I'll incorporate are cheeses, spices, chiles, and bourbon. Smoked Gouda and charred jalapeños create a wood-fired profile in the mac and cheese recipe, while still maintaining an extra creamy bite of perfectly cooked pasta. The roasted flavors of the *Arizona Adobo Sauce* add a depth of fire to the *Desert Deviled Eggs* while allowing each bite to stay vibrant and refreshing. As you're preparing side dishes for barbecue, think about the balance of flavors on the plate and how you can bring the char without overpowering the tongue.

CRISPY
SKILLET POTATOES
WITH MOJO ROJO AND MOJO VERDE

Chef José Andrés inspired me with his recipe for *papas arrugadas*: salted potatoes served with a vibrant Spanish mojo verde. I often find vibrant sauces are key to grilled foods, brightening the charred and smoky flavors. Here, we keep the potatoes simple and pair them with two sauces, swapping out the chiles as the main ingredients. Sweet red bell pepper and guajillos create a smoky, sweet sauce that has a mild heat. Roasted green bell pepper and serrano are paired with cilantro for a vibrant, sharp bite of spice. Red wine vinegar, garlic, and oil bond the ingredients into a creamy, emulsified explosion of flavor. Serve them up and let guests choose which sauce they want—though I strongly recommend a splash of both.

MOJO VERDE SAUCE

1 green bell pepper

1 serrano chile

1 small bunch fresh cilantro with stems

1 teaspoon ground cumin

3 garlic cloves, chopped

2 tablespoons (28 ml) red wine vinegar

⅓ cup (80 ml) extra-virgin olive oil

1 teaspoon sea salt

MOJO ROJO SAUCE

1 red bell pepper

2 dried guajillo chiles, stemmed and seeded

1 teaspoon smoked paprika

3 garlic cloves, chopped

2 teaspoons red wine vinegar

⅓ cup (80 ml) extra-virgin olive oil

1 teaspoon sea salt

POTATOES

2 pounds (900 g) Yukon Gold baby potatoes

3 tablespoons (45 ml) olive oil

1 teaspoon kosher salt

½ teaspoon fresh ground black pepper

½ cup (120 ml) water

INSTRUCTIONS

Preheat the grill for direct cooking at medium heat, 300–350°F (150–180°C). Clean the grill grates and oil them as needed.

Place the green bell pepper, serrano chile, red bell pepper, and the guajillo chiles directly over the flames. The guajillos will darken and puff up quickly, so remove them after they start to toast for about ➤➤

30 seconds on each side. Char the other peppers until their skin is dark and blistered. Remove them and place all the peppers in a plastic bag or a sealed container to steam and soften.

Slice the baby potatoes in half lengthwise, placing them in a large bowl. Add the olive oil, salt, and pepper to the potatoes and mix well to evenly coat.

Place a large skillet or a grill-safe pan on the grill. Make sure this pan has a lid, so we can steam the potatoes. Add the seasoned potatoes with ½ cup (120 ml) of water. Place the lid on and allow to cook for 20–25 minutes, stirring halfway.

Prepare the sauces while the potatoes cook. Stem, seed, and peel the charred chiles. Add the red bell pepper and the guajillo into a blender with the rest of the ingredients for the *Mojo Rojo Sauce* and purée until smooth. Set aside and repeat with the green bell pepper, serrano chile, and the rest of the ingredients for the *Mojo Verde Sauce*. Taste each and adjust with salt as needed.

Check the potatoes with a fork to see if they are tender, adding a little more water and time if not. When they are tender, go ahead and remove the lid, allowing them to fry in their oil. Continue cooking over the fire for 5–8 minutes until they are perfectly crispy on the outside.

Remove the skillet from the heat. Serve the warm potatoes with one or both sauces.

PICO DE GALLO SALAD
WITH LIME VINAIGRETTE

SERVES
4–5
PEOPLE

Sometimes, you just need a fresh side alongside the smoky piles of barbecue. *Pico de Gallo Salad* is a simple side with familiar flavors. Biting into a juicy gem of a cherry tomato that has soaked up the vinaigrette is exciting—and it's the perfect size to contain all of those flavors. The addition of avocado adds a creamy, fatty component to counter the acid from the tomatoes and vinaigrette. Jalapeños add a contrasting bitter flavor, and red pepper flakes reinforce that spicy punch with a little crunch. Try pairing this with grilled steaks, chicken, or tacos.

PICO DE GALLO SALAD

1 pint (473 ml) cherry tomatoes

1–2 jalapeño peppers, plus more as needed

1 cup (160 g) diced red onion

2 avocados, cubed

2 tablespoons (12 g) chopped fresh mint

2 tablespoons (2 g) chopped fresh cilantro

LIME VINAIGRETTE

Juice of 2 limes

2 tablespoons (28 ml) olive oil, plus more as needed

2 tablespoons (2 g) chopped fresh cilantro

½ teaspoon kosher salt, plus more as needed

½ teaspoon fresh ground black pepper

½ teaspoon red pepper flakes

INSTRUCTIONS

Slice the cherry tomatoes in half. Remove the stems and seeds of the jalapeño pepper(s) and finely dice. Taste to determine the heat and add more if desired. Add the tomatoes and jalapeños to a salad bowl along with the red onion, avocado, mint, and cilantro.

Prepare the vinaigrette. In a small bowl, mix the ingredients with a whisk or a fork to combine. Taste and adjust. Add more oil if it's too acidic or more salt if it needs more definition.

Pour the *Lime Vinaigrette* over the salad, gently toss, and season with salt as needed. You can prepare this salad ahead of time but keep the vinaigrette on the side until ready to serve.

NOTE: You may use 4 cups (656 g) of frozen corn kernels, making sure they are completely thawed and drained of excess water. Freshly grated Parmesan cheese can be substituted for the Cotija cheese if not available. Just be aware that both Parmesan and Cotija cheese are salty, so take that into consideration when seasoning your corn.

SOUTHWEST
CREAMED CORN

MAKES
ABOUT

4
CUPS

Mexican street corn pairs perfectly with barbeque. You get the fresh flavors of summer with the cooling cream and cheese in every bite. Fresh corn on the cob isn't always available, but my desire to eat it is ever-present. Transforming the flavors into one of my favorite sides, creamed corn, has been a huge hit at parties over the years. I consider it an ode to both my Midwest upbringing and my penchant for Southwest spice. Earthy poblanos are sautéed with garlic to provide some contrast to the sweet corn. Serve this warm dish with any grilled meat, eat with tortilla chips and salsa, or spoon on top of nachos.

8 medium ears corn, husk and silk
    removed (about 4 cups [616 g])
3 tablespoons (42 g) butter
2 tablespoons (16 g) all-purpose flour
3 garlic cloves, minced
¼ cup (30 g) diced poblano chiles
½ teaspoon kosher salt
½ teaspoon black pepper
½ teaspoon paprika
1 tablespoon (13 g) sugar
1 cup (235 ml) heavy cream
Juice of 1 lime

FOR GARNISH
1 cup (120 g) Cotija cheese
¼ cup (4 g) chopped fresh cilantro
1 tablespoon (7 g) paprika or (8 g)
    Spicy Chili Powder (page 31)

INSTRUCTIONS

Using a small paring knife, carefully slice the corn kernels from the cobs into a large bowl. Using the back of the knife, scrape off any juices from the cob.

Heat a saucepan over medium heat. Add the butter and flour, whisking to cook out the raw flavor of the flour. After about 2 minutes, add the garlic and poblano chiles and stir, mixing for about 2 minutes.

Add the corn kernels, salt, pepper, paprika, and sugar. Cook and stir for another 3–4 minutes until the corn is completely coated.

Add the heavy cream and cook for another 10–15 minutes until it has thickened and the corn is cooked through. Stir frequently, as the cream might start to bubble. Remove the pan from the heat and stir in the lime juice and ½ cup (60 g) of the Cotija cheese. Taste and adjust.

Garnish with the remaining Cotija cheese, chopped cilantro, and paprika. Serve while warm.

LEMON-SERRANO GRILLED
SUMMER SQUASH

SERVES
3–5
PEOPLE

Chef Pati Jinich shared a captivating condiment on her show while filming in Cancún: serrano chiles marinated with lemon juice and olive oil. It's a vibrant combination with fresh flavors and a surprisingly strong, sharp heat from the serranos. Using this over the years, I discovered that grilled vegetables are a perfect match, the oil and acid creating a perfect baste for grilling hot and fast. Summer squash can be quickly grilled while your meat is resting, only taking a few minutes to char. The salty Cotija cheese is a perfect garnish, seasoning the veggies and complementing the lemon flavor. Feel free to swap it for feta, queso fresco, or even goat cheese.

INGREDIENTS

1 serrano chile, seeded and
thinly sliced
2 tablespoons (28 ml) fresh lemon
juice, plus more as needed
¼ cup (60 ml) olive oil
¼ teaspoon kosher salt, plus more
as needed
1 pound (455 g) summer squash
varieties (zucchini, yellow
crookneck, etc.)
½ cup (60 g) Cotija cheese

INSTRUCTIONS

In a small bowl, mix the serrano chile, lemon juice, olive oil, and salt. Taste and adjust with more salt or lemon juice as needed. Allow it to marinate for at least an hour. The oil will draw out the heat from the serrano and become quite spicy.

Preheat the grill for direct cooking at high heat, 400–450°F (200–230°C). Clean the grill grates and oil them as needed. The squash tends to absorb anything left behind.

Slice the squash into slices about ¼ inch (6 mm) or slightly thicker. Diagonal slices are the best, giving more surface area, and they look nice. Place the slices in a large bowl and drizzle some of the lemon-serrano oil over the top, stirring gently to ensure they are coated evenly.

Grill the squash over direct heat for 3–4 minutes per side until they are almost cooked through. You should see some char and grill marks, and the squash will be very tender but not mushy.

Remove them from the grill and toss with additional lemon-serrano oil to taste. Garnish with the salty Cotija cheese and serve immediately.

CREAMY DIJON HERB
SLAW

MAKES
ABOUT

8

CUPS
(960 G)

Every good outdoor barbecue needs a slaw. My tangy rendition has both sour cream and *Smoked Garlic Aioli*, a perfect base to elevate any lean meat such as grilled shrimp, fish, or chicken. There are definitely tricks to making a vibrant, crispy, and creamy slaw. Draining the cabbage of excess liquid ensures that the dressing remains creamy and not watery. Slowly adding the dressing to the vegetables to get the perfect coating with every bite is also important. But I think the fresh dill is the key to this slaw, as it brightens every crunchy bite.

INGREDIENTS

6 cups (420 g) shredded white
   cabbage
1 teaspoons kosher salt, plus more
   as needed
¼ cup (60 g) *Smoked Garlic Aioli*
   (page 37)
¼ cup (60 g) sour cream
¼ cup (60 ml) apple cider vinegar
¼ cup (60 g) Dijon mustard
2 tablespoons (26 g) white sugar
1 large white onion, finely sliced
2 medium-size carrots, peeled and cut
   into matchsticks
2 celery stalks, peeled and diced
2 tablespoons (8 g) chopped fresh dill
1 teaspoon fresh ground black pepper
2 teaspoons red pepper flakes
   (optional)

INSTRUCTIONS

Place the shredded cabbage in a colander over a bowl, toss it with the salt, and let it rest for 1–2 hours, tossing occasionally. Gently squeeze out the water from the cabbage, which will help keep the cabbage crisp for much longer.

In a small bowl, stir together the *Smoked Garlic Aioli*, sour cream, apple cider vinegar, Dijon mustard, and sugar to mix the dressing. In a large bowl, combine the cabbage, onion, carrots, celery, and dill. Mix in the dressing a little bit at a time while stirring the vegetables together. This helps you coat the ingredients while making sure there's not too much dressing. Season with pepper and add red pepper flakes, if desired, and additional salt as needed.

Let the flavors meld together in the fridge for a couple of hours before serving. This slaw will stay fresh for 2–4 days, especially if you drained the water from the cabbage.

NOTE: I recommend using filtered apple cider vinegar, not "from the mother." Mix up the flavor profiles by testing out different acids and herbs. Chopped cilantro and fresh poblano strips with lime juice makes an excellent southwest version.

CHIPOTLE BACON
TWICE-BAKED POTATOES

Growing up in a Midwest family means that twice-baked potatoes are usually showing up at the party. My mom would always set some aside in the fridge, knowing that these were my favorite leftovers. If you've never had the pleasure: Baked potatoes are scooped out and mashed with a classic combination of sour cream and cheese; however, my recipe is also fortified with chopped chipotles and scallions. Spicy, creamy, and smoky flavors pair well with pretty much any type of barbecue.

MAKES
10
TWICE-BAKED POTATOES
ENOUGH FOR 6–8 PEOPLE

INGREDIENTS

5 russet potatoes, rinsed and scrubbed
2 tablespoons (28 ml) olive oil
2 sticks (1 cup, or 225 g) salted butter
1 cup (230 g) sour cream
2 garlic cloves, grated
6 chipotle chiles in adobo, minced
2 tablespoons (30 g) adobo sauce from the chipotle chiles
1½ cups (173 g) shredded Monterey Jack cheese
3 scallions, sliced thin
Kosher salt
3–4 tablespoons (15 to 20 g) *Smoky Bacon Crumble* (page 165)

INSTRUCTIONS

Prepare the smoker or grill for indirect cooking at 400°F (200°C). Mesquite or hickory wood pairs well with the flavors. If using a grill, prepare a 2-zone cooking setup, with the hot coals on one side. Clean the grill grates and oil them as needed.

Wash and dry the potatoes. Using a fork, poke a few holes in the top of each one and rub with a little of the olive oil. This will help the skin crisp. Cook the potatoes for about an hour, until they are cooked through and slightly soft when squeezed. Remove the potatoes when ready and lower the heat of the smoker to 350°F (180°C).

Slice the butter into pats and place in a large bowl, along with the sour cream, garlic, chipotle chiles, and adobo sauce.

Carefully cut eat baked potato in half lengthwise. Scrape out the insides, leaving a rib of potato inside the skin for support. Lay the hollowed-out skins on a baking sheet.

Smash the potato filling in the bowl with the rest of the ingredients. Mix in 1 cup (115 g) of Monterey Jack cheese, scallions, and salt to taste. Generously add the filling to each of the potato skins, which should be a heaping pile for each one. Top each one with the remaining Monterey Jack cheese.

Cook the potatoes on the baking sheet for 10–15 minutes until the cheese has completely melted and started to crisp on the top. Finish them off with a dusting of *Smoky Bacon Crumble* and serve.

SKILLET-ROASTED
MUSHROOMS
WITH SPICY GARLIC BUTTER

<table>
<tr><td>

SERVES

4–6

PEOPLE

</td><td>

Mushrooms deserve a bigger spotlight. Cooked properly, they are bursting with a natural, beefy flavor. Tossing them with a savory butter sauce really helps, so that's what's happening here. These skillet-roasted mushrooms are crispy on the outside, tender on the inside, and dressed with rich spicy garlic butter. Try pairing them with *Coffee-Rubbed Tri-tip with Shishito Gremolata* (page 69) and *Southwest Creamed Corn* (page 173) for a well-rounded, flavorful dinner table.

</td></tr>
</table>

MUSHROOMS

2 pounds (900 g) whole mushrooms, cremini or button

2 tablespoons (28 ml) olive oil

½ teaspoon kosher salt

½ teaspoon black pepper

SPICY GARLIC BUTTER

1 tablespoon (14 g) unsalted butter

3 garlic cloves, grated

1 teaspoon *Spicy Chili Powder* (page 31)

¼ cup (55 g) unsalted butter, at room temperature

Kosher salt

FOR GARNISH

½ cup (30 g) chopped fresh parsley or (8 g) cilantro

INSTRUCTIONS

Prepare the smoker or grill for indirect cooking at 375°F (190°C). If using a grill, prepare a 2-zone cooking setup, with the hot coals on one side.

Prepare the mushrooms by trimming, washing, and patting them dry. In a large bowl, toss the whole mushrooms with the olive oil, salt, and pepper. Place them in a large skillet, spreading them out in an even layer as much as possible. Set the skillet inside the grill or smoker and allow them to cook for 15 minutes with the lid closed.

After 15 minutes, check the mushrooms. Carefully drain the excess liquid from the bottom of the skillet and place it back inside the grill for another 30 minutes with the lid closed.

Meanwhile, prepare the butter. In a small pan, melt the tablespoon (14 g) of butter over medium heat. Add the garlic and *Spicy Chili Powder*, stirring to cook the garlic for about 2 minutes. Remove from the heat and pour it into a bowl, allowing it to cool to room temperature. Mash in the remaining ¼ cup (55 g) of room-temperature butter and taste. Add salt if needed. Set the garlic butter aside.

Check on the mushrooms after the final 30 minutes. They should be darker, much smaller, and the liquid should be mostly gone from the bottom of the skillet. Remove the skillet from the grill and add a spoonful of the *Spicy Garlic Butter*, tossing to coat the mushrooms. Indulge and add more butter because it tastes incredible, and you went through the effort. Garnish with chopped fresh herbs and serve immediately.

ROASTED
SWEET POTATOES
WITH GOCHUJANG BUTTER

MAKES

4

**SWEET
POTATOES**

Spicy and sweet butter can make just about any dish special, especially roasted sweet potatoes. Originally, this recipe for *Gochujang Butter* was used for pork chops. One day, I was serving the chops with sweet potatoes, and it just made sense to double down with the flavors. Baking sweet potatoes with wood-fired flavors adds a smoky depth to the outside while caramelizing the inside. Deep, nutty flavors come alive with a healthy dollop of salted, spicy *Gochujang Butter* infused with honey. Pair this with any grilled steak, chicken, or pork for an instant hit. The butter goes on everything, especially the *Coffee-Rubbed Tri-tip with Shishito Gremolata* (page 69) or the *Skillet-Roasted Mushrooms* (page 181).

4 sweet potatoes, orange variety

GOCHUJANG BUTTER
2 sticks (1 cup, or 225 g) unsalted
    butter, at room temperature
2 tablespoons (30 g) gochujang
1 scallion, chopped
2 garlic cloves, peeled
1 teaspoon honey
½ teaspoon kosher salt, plus more
    as needed

FOR GARNISH
4 tablespoons (12 g) chopped chives
Sesame seeds

INSTRUCTIONS

Prepare the smoker or grill for indirect cooking at 400°F (200°C). If using a grill, prepare a 2-zone cooking setup, with the hot coals on one side. Clean the grill grates and oil them as needed.

Scrub and clean the sweet potatoes. Poke a few holes in the top with a fork. Place in the smoker or grill and allow to cook for at least 50 minutes, checking to see if they are cooked. They will be ready when they are between 205–210°F (96–99°C) internal temperature, which might take longer if they are larger.

Prepare the compound butter while the potatoes cook. Add all of the ingredients to a food processor. Mix on low speed to fully combine all ingredients. Taste and add more salt as needed. Transfer the compound butter to a container and set aside.

Once the potatoes are ready, remove them from the grill or smoker. Split the potatoes down the middle and spoon in a healthy amount of *Gochujang Butter*. Garnish with the chopped chives and sesame seeds and serve immediately.

RESOURCES

COWBOY CHARCOAL (*cowboycharcoal.com*)
Cowboy Charcoal specializes in charcoal briquettes and lump charcoal, both quick lighting and long lasting. It's important to have consistency when working with fire, which is what I've found while using this brand. I also appreciate the different types of woods used in their charcoal lineup.

FINEX (*finexusa.com*)
This is the highest-quality cast-iron cookware that I've worked with. Not only do their products look amazing, with their sharp angles, but they are also incredibly functional and nearly nonstick right out of the box. The spiral handles are a game changer, keeping the heat away for as long as possible.

MELISSA'S PRODUCE (*melissas.com*)
Certain vegetables and fruits are harder to find, but Melissa's carries just about everything you can imagine. Their specialty is their abundant stock of seasonal produce, always up to date with plenty of online resources for recipes.

SPICEOLOGY (*spiceology.com*)
Having the freshest chiles, dried herbs, and spices make a world of difference when cooking. Spiceology grinds everything in small batches, shipping directly to the consumer rather than having product sitting on shelves at big box stores. Everything they bottle has bolder, fresher flavors.

THERMOWORKS (*thermoworks.com*)
Find one of the most important tools for a griller right here. ThermoWorks has the most reliable thermometers for cooking that I've come across, no matter the product you're cooking. I recommend their Thermapen for grilling and smoke setup for ongoing monitoring while smoking.

WESTERN PREMIUM BBQ PRODUCTS (*westernbbqproducts.com*)
Wood chunks and wood chips are important components when adding smoke flavor to food over the fire, or in the smoker. Western has a large variety of wood types available in both chips and chunks, online and in many local stores.

WILDWOOD GRILLING (wildwoodgrilling.com)
Wildwood Grilling carries the largest selection of wood grilling planks, such as cedar, hickory, and red oak. Their wood is high quality, smells great, and is never dry or cracking. Available both online and in stores.

ACKNOWLEDGMENTS

THIS BOOK COULD NOT HAVE HAPPENED without many trials, successes, and the support of so many. I will do my best to thank everyone involved over the years.

First, I want to thank Jesus who has generously blessed our family through this journey. Nothing would be possible without your grace and guidance.

To my loving wife, Yarizeth, who has shown me limitless support since the beginning. I appreciate your comfort when I've failed, your patience when I've been cooking and cleaning for days, and your feedback when I needed honesty. Thank you for listening, regardless of the time of day. You've always believed in me, fueling the passion behind *Chiles and Smoke*.

To my two sons, Braxton and Zachariah. You are too young in this moment to understand how much I appreciate the unconditional support and cheer. You've painted me into the picture of a hero, and it has kept me motivated through my deepest struggles. I can't wait until you're old enough to read this book, which was written as a food-legacy for you.

To those who have inspired me and invested time in me. Derek Wolf, thank you for believing in my work enough to recommend and consult me along the way. It's a blessing to have found a brother in barbecue. Thank you, Matt Deaton, for your time helping me troubleshoot the menu and the ongoing encouragement throughout the entire process. Friends like Kita Roberts, Merry Graham, Jeremy Whitelaw, Sam Bricca, and Misty Banchero, for all of the times you've had to sit there and listen as I brainstormed. Thank you for pushing me in the directions I needed, even if it's not what I wanted to hear. You are all amazing friends.

To my Cookbook Crew, the team of cooks and chefs who helped make this book possible. Chef Stephanie Hamilton, Nicole Stover, Danielle Cochran, and Kevin Reeves, I appreciate all of your time and feedback as we cooked our way through this book together. Your input has helped me become a better cook, writer, and photographer along the way. Thank you to Tayunaz Merchant, my chef consultant on many international dishes throughout the book. I appreciate your time, attention to details, and helping me find my voice while respecting authenticity.

Lastly, thank you to those who have followed my journey through the website, social media, and more. You make a difference and are one of the biggest reasons I've been able to do this. Thank you to the many more who should be named, knowing that I am grateful.

ABOUT THE AUTHOR

BRAD PROSE is a professional recipe developer, food writer, and culinary photographer. He is the founder and force behind Chiles and Smoke, a website dedicated to inspire readers to use new flavor combinations, techniques, and ingredients when grilling or smoking. His combined passion for fine dining and BBQ shines through his presentations and cooking style. Making his mark in the wide world of BBQ, Brad produces high-quality, unique recipes to challenge and expand the home cook's comfort zone. He has cooked on *LIVE* with Kelly and Ryan, published recipes for BBQGuys, *Tailgater Magazine*, and many other publications. You can keep up to date with his work on social media and on his website: chilesandsmoke.com.

RECIPES BY CHILE INDEX

	JALAPENOS	CHIPOTLES	SERRANOS	GUAJILLO	ANCHO	KOREAN CHILES	HATCH CHILES	CHILE DE ARBOL	SHISHITOS	BELL PEPPERS	HABANERO	POBLANOS
BRISKET, BEEF, BURGERS & LAMB												
Chiles and Smoke Burger	✓											
Gochujang Chili Con Carne	✓	✓				✓						
Smoked Sonoran Chili	✓	✓		✓	✓							
Sonoran "Red Hots"	✓	✓		✓	✓							
Smoked Harissa Beef Tacos		✓		✓								
Coffee-Rubbed Tritip with Shishito Gremolata					✓				✓			
Firecracker Brisket												
Garlic Mojo Skirt Steak Tacos	✓	✓										
Planked Jalapeno Bourbon Meatloaf with Guajillo Bourbon Glaze	✓			✓								
Vindaloo-Spiced Lamb Lollipops	✓							✓				
Smoked Lamb Barbacoa Banh Mi	✓			✓	✓						✓	
Shishito Cheesesteak Queso									✓	✓		
Big Beef Ribs with Barbacoa Sauce		✓		✓	✓							
WINGS, TINGA & OTHER CHICKEN DISHES												
Chipotle Tahini Grilled Chicken		✓										
Tandoori butterflied Chicken Drumsticks				✓								
Nashville Hot BBQ Chicken		✓		✓	✓							
Grilled Adobo-Rubbed Chicken with Creamy Herb Sauce				✓	✓							
Grilled Chicken Tinga	✓			✓	✓							
Grilled Chicken Fajita Wedge Salad		✓		✓	✓					✓		
Gochujang Honey Mustard Chicken Sandwich						✓				✓		
Enchilada Wings				✓	✓			✓				
Spicy Orange Chicken Wings						✓						
Bacon-Wrapped Cheesy Chicken Poblanos	✓											✓
RIBS, CHORIZO & EVERYTHING PORK												
Crispy Pork Belly with Red Chimichurri		✓			✓					✓		
Chipotle Pork Belly Burnt Ends with Jalapeno Berry Sauce	✓	✓										
Smoked Pork Steaks with Harissa Habanero Butter		✓		✓								
Smoked Ancho-Orange Pulled Pork				✓	✓							
Chile Verde Baby Back Ribs	✓	✓			✓							✓

	JALAPENOS	CHIPOTLES	SERRANOS	GUAJILLO	ANCHO	KOREAN CHILES	HATCH CHILES	CHILE DE ARBOL	SHISHITOS	BELL PEPPERS	HABANERO	POBLANOS
RIBS, CHORIZO & EVERYTHING PORK (CONT.)												
Smoked Chorizo Meatballs		✓										
Roasted Chile Meatball Hero	✓	✓										
Grilled Pork Tenderloin Al Pastor	✓		✓	✓				✓				
HALIBUT, SCALLOPS, SHRIMP, SALMON & MORE												
Corn Husk-Wrapped Halibut with Jalapeno Basil Butter	✓											
Summer BBQ Grilled Scallops and Corn		✓		✓	✓							
Huli Huli Shrimp, Shishito and Pineapple Skewers	✓							✓				
Hatch Chile Smoked Shrimp Skillet		✓		✓	✓		✓					
Spicy Grilled California Crab-Stuffed Avocados												
Tandoori Grilled Lobster with Lemon Parsley Aioli				✓								
Planked Pomegranate Harissa Salmon		✓		✓								
SALADS, SIDES & VEGETABLE MAIN DISHES												
Creamy Dijon Herb Slaw												
Desert Deviled Eggs	✓			✓	✓							
Southwest Creamed Corn												✓
Harissa Sweet Potato Salad		✓		✓								
Creamy Jalapeno Popper Mac and Cheese	✓	✓		✓	✓							
Crispy Skillet Potatoes with Mojo Rojo and Verde			✓	✓						✓		
Lemon Serrano Grilled Summer Squash			✓									
Pico De Gallo Salad w/ Avocado and Mint	✓											
Skillet Roasted Mushrooms with Spicy Garlic Butter		✓		✓				✓				
Roasted Sweet Potatoes with Gochujang Butter						✓						
Chipotle Bacon Twice Baked Potatoes		✓										
SPICE RUBS & SAUCES												
Fresh Chili Powders		✓		✓	✓			✓				
Smoky Coffee Rub				✓								
Brad's Smoke Rub		✓		✓								
Smoked Garlic Aioli												
Guajillo Ketchup			✓									
Pickled Sweet Peppers										✓		
Arizona Adobo Sauce				✓	✓							
Brazilian Vinaigrette Salsa										✓		
Pickled Jalapenos	✓											
Smoky Southwest Harissa		✓		✓								
Charred Poblano Pico De Gallo	✓											✓
Hot Pickled Red Onions											✓	

INDEX